Am I Alone in Thinking…?

Am I Alone in Thinking...?

Unpublished Letters to
The Daily Telegraph

EDITED BY
IAIN HOLLINGSHEAD

First published in Great Britain
2009 by Aurum Press Ltd
7 Greenland Street
London NW1 0ND
www.aurumpress.co.uk

A catalogue record for this book is available from the
British Library.

ISBN 978 1 84513 502 7

10 9 8 7 6 5 4 3 2 1
2013 2012 2011 2010 2009

Text design in Mrs Eaves by Roger Hammond
Printed by MPG Books, Ltd, Bodmin, Cornwall

SIR – I am sure that all of your highly paid journalists are extremely intelligent and very well educated. Why is it, then, that when I long for an erudite, informed and beautifully expressed opinion, I turn first to the Letters to the Editor?

Margaret Long
Devizes, Somerset

SIR – Any chance of having a page or two of your surplus Letters to the Editor published? With the limiting factor of space in your daily paper there must be a wealth of humour, information and points of view just thrown away. Such a waste!

Barrie Yelland
Helston, Cornwall

SIR – Am I the only one who is irritated by the number of your correspondents who start their letters by asking if they are the only one?

Geoff Hill
Wrington, Somerset

CONTENTS

INTRODUCTION

When children grow up dreaming about becoming journalists – if, indeed, children do still grow up with such dreams – I doubt their fantasies include working on a Letters Desk. Surely journalism is about big scoops (duck houses spring to mind), hard-hitting interviews, in-depth features, foreign travel, free tickets to football matches . . . it is not about sifting through green-ink-flecked correspondence from the aggrieved, the bored, the lonely, the pushy and the borderline insane (not that *Telegraph* readers fit these stereotypes, of course) in a desperate bid to cobble together a coherent Letters page.

Certainly, a life in letters appears to compare unfavourably at first glance with the glamorous existence of Carl Bernstein, Bob Woodward or even William Boot. At *The Daily Telegraph*, two people click through approximately 500 emails every day (they may be called "Letters to the Editor"; a more accurate title would be "Emails to the Letters Editors") and choose, edit and collate around 20 to publish in the paper. On sunny days, when our traditional readership can be found enjoying their gardens (before returning indoors to send us an email about a rare type of goldfinch they've spotted), the volume decreases noticeably. However, when the really important news stories break – I refer, of course, to Carol Thatcher saying the word golliwog or John Sergeant leaving *Strictly Come Dancing* – our inbox bursts to overflowing.

During the MPs' expenses scandal, the tally was touching 1,500 daily. Every single one is read and carefully considered, even if it repeats the same joke we've heard a dozen times before lunch.

On top of our electronic postbag, we receive around 100 faxes every day and a similar number of letters by post. One strange individual sends us a suspiciously squidgy jiffy bag at regular intervals. Although our long-suffering secretary, Dorothy Brown, has become an expert at spotting the postmark and confining the putrid package to the bin, we'd be grateful if the Bristol resident in question could find somewhere else to relieve himself.

Yet despite these minor setbacks, *The Daily Telegraph's* Letters Desk, perhaps more than any of its rivals, is a truly wonderful place to work. The sheer volume of (non-organic) material we receive means that discovering the many gems from our diverse and intelligent readership makes it well worth sifting through some of the spoil.

Over the year I've worked full-time on the desk, covering the maternity leave of Matilda McLean, the Deputy Letters Editor, we've published letters from the likes of Frederick Forsyth, the Archbishop of Canterbury, Colin Firth, Scarlett Johansson and, perhaps less gloriously, David Blunkett, whose regular streams of consciousness require more translation than most. But what really makes the page so special is that it belongs to the ordinary readers; it is a space where they can set the agenda, contributing unmatched expertise and insight from their own, very varied experiences. For example, every time there's an article in the paper about defence cuts, dozens of senior officers write the same day with their own contrasting views. Likewise teaching; policing; medicine; finance. Someone, somewhere, among our readership of more than two million will have an informed opinion. The page is a daily tribute to the wisdom of crowds, a judiciously edited form of "citizen journalism" at its best.

It is also a tribute to the generosity of our readers. Last December, we published a letter from someone who felt lonely at Christmas. Enough cards were sent to him via the *Telegraph* to fill all his windowsills and most of his walls. He wrote again in gratitude. In spring this year, a carer of a former Japanese Prisoner of War described his charge's stoicism in facing an impoverished retirement. Several thousand pounds were subsequently sent in donations, enabling the carer to double-glaze all the PoW's windows to help keep out the cold.

The letters we publish can also offer a delightful change of tone amid the more serious Comment pages. Over the course of a couple of weeks in May this year, readers tracked the mass migration of a rabble of painted lady butterflies from the Isle of Wight to the north of Scotland. The correspondence was eventually put to rest by Damian Whitehead, writing from Gosport in Hampshire: "During my naval career, I saw painted ladies in Bugis Street, Singapore. However, they were not butterflies and some of them were certainly not ladies."

Telegraph readers are a witty demographic. Some of the most enjoyable – and long-running – recent correspondences have been on such diverse topics as the perils of losing your spouse in a supermarket, the strange names we give to our houses and the correct way to eat marmalade at breakfast. As Valerie Shepherd from Sarisbury Green in Hampshire wrote: "It was interesting to discover, while holidaying on a Turkish *gulet* last week, just how many times I referred to one of your readers' letters to contribute to conversation round the table."

Hosting this ongoing international conversation, expertly deciding when to move it on or nudge it in a different direction, is Christopher Howse, the Letters Editor and one of the wisest, most interesting (and most bearded) people I have ever met. A reader has no more chance of sneaking a misquotation, a misplaced semi-colon or a hoary old chestnut past Christopher than Simon Heffer has of writing for the *Guardian*. Edit letters badly and they read like a mess of shouted, misshapen rants – much like many of the comments below blogs. Edit them well and there is a sense of direction, debate – even community.

Fortunately, I don't think I am alone in believing that our readers have created one of the finest – if not *the* finest – Letters pages in the world. When Tony Blair trumped Gordon Brown, again, by becoming the first world statesman to shake hands with President Obama, the former Prime Minister mentioned that he had read the *"Telegraph's* famous letters page" at the airport and had been reminded of his relative unpopularity in Britain (the letter in question spoke of Blair's lack of intelligence compared to Cherie's). More prosaically, a fresh copy of our letters is hung daily above the urinals in a Westminster pub called St Stephen's Tavern. They are also regularly spoofed in the fictional form of Sir Herbert Gussett in *Private Eye*.

It was during our month-long exposure of MPs' expenses, which set the news agenda in Britain and made headlines around the world, that readers' letters really came into their own. On the first day, we gave the entire page over to their views – the first time that this had been done in the *Telegraph's* history. It stayed this way for the next fortnight as thousands of angry, erudite and witty ordinary people made their opinions felt. The *Today* programme regularly read out the best ones. Ian Hislop even quoted from the "brilliant *Telegraph's* letters page" on *Have I Got News for You*.

As the volume of letters increased, so necessarily did the ones we couldn't publish. Realising this, a couple of readers began to suggest that we publish a book of previously unpublished letters. Barrie Yelland's enthusiasm for the idea prefaces this book. "What a magnificent, humorous and salutary publication that would be," agreed Dr A.W. Taylor from Oldham in Lancashire. "The wit it would contain would render it the only item required for many joyful years on an MP-free desert island."

Such unexpected support was hugely encouraging, because I had already been working quietly on exactly this idea for over a year. In my first week of occasional shifts on the Letters Desk, back in March 2008, I was immediately struck by the quality of many of the letters for which we didn't have space. Often, some of the best ones never made the page as they arrived too late and the news agenda had moved on, or they addressed an interesting topic which didn't quite fit with the rest of the day's selection. Sometimes, they were a little too whimsical, or indeed too risqué, for a serious daily newspaper. Sometimes, they were too lowbrow for Christopher's tastes. Sometimes, frankly, they were completely and utterly (and wonderfully) mad. One of my favourite correspondents, who you will see cropping up intermittently throughout the book, believes himself to be the head of MI6, and writes regularly with his unique take on the day's news, identifying himself only as "M". The impact is only slightly spoiled by his email footer, which reveals him to be writing from an internet café in Bristol (what is it about Bristol, I wonder?).

Whether late, whimsical or risqué – what all the best unpublished letters have in common is a unique, almost indefinable characteristic which convinced me that they merited a wider audience than a smile or two on the Letters Desk. So the book you are now holding is a collation of the best unpublished letters – of which there must have been more than 300,000 – submitted with the intention of publication over the last year and a half. This is not an anthology of mad letters – you should see some of the ones that libel laws sadly prohibit us from sharing – still less a B-side of the best of the rest. All the correspondents in the chapters that follow have entertaining and valid points to make on anyone and anything from Lord Mandelson to Madonna, cricket to the credit crunch, sex education to swine flu. I might not agree with some of their views – and neither necessarily, of course, does *The Daily Telegraph* – but I do believe they deserve a voice.

While there are a handful of phrases that soon grow wearisome to any letters editor – *It's political correctness gone mad; the lunatics really have taken over the asylum; the health and safety fascists; I could go on; I rest my case* – I continue to find something rather touching about people wondering if they are alone in thinking the way they do and sitting down to write to a newspaper to test the water. In an age of sometimes bewildering and often alienating change, it is reassuring to think that something as seemingly old-fashioned as a Letters page can still provide a focal point for readers to connect with others. They need howl into the void no longer. They are not alone.

Iain Hollingshead
The Daily Telegraph
London SW1
July 2009

ACKNOWLEDGEMENTS

I would like to express my sincere gratitude to all our wonderful correspondents, without whom there would be no Letters page, no book and probably no *Daily Telegraph* either. Although in the course of a normal day on the desk we rarely have time to reply to anyone beyond an automated acknowledgement, we soon feel that we know the regulars – their prose style, their pet subjects, their idiosyncrasies. It has been a pleasure to correspond more directly with some of them during the course of compiling this book. There are a few for whom only initials are given in the chapters that follow – either to spare their blushes or because, sadly, we didn't have a full address to get in touch.

I would also like to thank Christopher for giving me a job, Matilda for having a baby, Dorothy and Alex for being such fun colleagues, Will Lewis, the editor of *The Daily Telegraph*, for saying yes, Caroline Buckland, the head of *Telegraph* books, for being so encouraging and enthusiastic, Richard Preston for some valuable editorial advice, the incomparable Matt Pritchett for his cover illustration and Graham Coster at Aurum publishers for taking us on so gamely. I do hope you all enjoy the book.

BRITAIN AND BRITISHNESS TODAY

MUSIC TO THE EARS

SIR – Am I alone in noticing the correlation between the loudness of the music emanating from a vehicle, the awfulness of such music and the necessity to wear a baseball cap?

J.S.
St Albans, Hertfordshire

SIR – Is it just me or am I the only person in the western world who found Michael Jackson's music insipid, his eccentricities tedious and his behaviour with children wholly inappropriate and distasteful?

Laurence Rowe
Erith, Kent

A NATION OF WIMPS AND WAGS

SIR – What a nation of wimps we have become. I was raised in the 1950s and 1960s when there was no central heating in houses. I remember having to scrape ice from the inside of windows many a time. The younger generation should be taught to dress more appropriately in the winter.

Ann Baxter
Bristol

SIR – As I read in the obituaries the fascinating story of yet another war-time hero who has sadly passed away, I wonder if, in 50 years time, all your future readers will have to read about are the exploits of *Big Brother* contestants and Wags?

Jane Bryan
Devizes, Wiltshire

SIR – Jade Goody and Alfie Patten are both human tragedies in their different ways.

To pick over the pieces we have Max Clifford. Am I the only one to find it a revolting scene?

Don Roberts
Prenton, Wirral

SIR – Perhaps 13-year-old Alfie Patten should join Fathers for Justice – he surely already owns a Spiderman outfit.

David Yexley
Boscombe Down, Wiltshire

SIR – In an odd moment of reverie the other day, a snatch of the old song "There'll Always Be an England" came unbidden into my mind.

I stood there and wept, for they were wrong.

Jasper R. Dimond
Burgess Hill, West Sussex

SIR – On Wednesday afternoon, under a hot sun, I saw a Spitfire overhead doing aerobatics. This is the only way I know to thank the pilot and his victory roll over our house – I cried.

Simon Moss
Lower Boddington, Northamptonshire

SIR – I lived and worked through the Second World War and never saw a fat person. If we had we would have questioned who was topping up that person's ration book.

Do we need another war to beat obesity? What a ghastly thought.

Cicely Williams
Penrhyn Bay, Conwy

SIR – The recent correspondence on public lavatories in your Letters Pages reminded me of the arrangements circa 1900 when factories were built on the sides of rivers.

The factory I was familiar with had lavatory facilities consisting of large planks of wood with appropriate holes, extended over the slow-moving mill race.

The only downside was for the ladies whose plank, suitably enclosed, was downstream from the men's. I am told that the men used to make small rafts on which to place burning "material", which was then floated downstream.

In that less litigious age the matter was treated

with good humour – unlike what would happen now with the plethora of industrial, sex discrimination and health and safety laws.

William G. Black
Belfast

SIR – As I sit here approaching the end of our holiday on the Mayan Riviera, my wife and I are frankly astonished at the complete overreaction of some of our compatriots over a supposed swine flu pandemic.

Many have received multiple text messages from Britain, panicking them into a state of near hysteria. There are young couples here begging for flights home based on hyperbole created by the 24-hour news media and well-meaning but ill-informed friends.

To the amazement of our younger fellow holidaymakers, the reaction of my wife and I was to order a large gin and tonic and reconfirm our dinner reservation.

C.J. Rawson
Burnley, Lancashire

THE NORTH / SOUTH DIVIDE

SIR – A few years ago I was visiting my father in his new home town of Selby, North Yorkshire. I popped into town for a haircut and the nice lady cutting my hair noted, "You're not from round 'ere, are ya luv?"

I agreed and said that I was from London.

In the corner an old man was sitting reading the *Racing Post*. He lowered a corner of the paper and announced loudly: "I've been to London, and it's f***** s***."

P.R.
London SW18

THE GUARDIAN / TELEGRAPH DIVIDE

SIR – I am sure you've received countless letters from Brits who are outraged by the treatment of Lewis Hamilton by the Formula One stewards. Therefore I will not add my own expressions of anger.

Rather, I offer evidence that the nation's unhappiness is well founded. In a moment of boredom I read the comments on the subject on the *Guardian* website (it's always good to see what the enemy is thinking). To my surprise the same levels of fury were being expressed at length.

Not only was I taken aback by their support for a fellow Brit, I was even more surprised that *Guardian* readers could summon the energy for such an outpouring of emotion, fuelled only by a diet of lentils and aubergine hot-pot.

Phil Bailey
Crickhowell, Powys

SIR – Oh dear me: there I was trying to improve my sad *Independent/Guardian* woolly liberal-cum-socialist mind by reading bits of your paper online, starting with readers' letters, and what did I get? Three religious leaders whose distrust of human nature is apparently so great that it leaves them unable to support any idea of allowing voluntary euthanasia to be added to the range of compassionate options already available for the terminally ill; and a vet who advocates thrashing cows for trying to protect their offspring from a domesticated wolf.

Alison Sutherland
St Ola, Orkney

SIR – The trouble with writing to the *Telegraph* is that, although it makes one feel better, it is really preaching to the converted. Perhaps we should seek to influence others by writing to the tabloids instead?

Martin Ranwell
Modbury, Devon

DID YOUR MANSERVANT PACK THIS BAG HIMSELF?

SIR – I find it intensely humiliating to be asked by airport security staff if I have packed my own bag. This forces one to admit, usually within earshot of others, that I no longer have a manservant to do the chore for me.

Gentlemen should be able to answer such questions with a disdainful: "Of course not! Do I look like that sort of person?"

Arthur W. J. G. Ord-Hume
Guildford, Surrey

SIR – It was with astonishment that I read your correspondent's claim that one doesn't throw bottles at one's servants in what he describes as a "regularly organised society". No doubt his domestic arrangements lack a certain *je ne sais quoi*, but he may take it from an old hand that a well-trained servant is virtually impossible to hit with a missile, however expertly aimed.

My own butler, for instance, is renowned for his fielding of the empty decanters I occasionally hurl at his head while fuming over my *Daily Telegraph*.

Glyn Palmer
Whitwell, Nottinghamshire

THE INTERNET
COUNTER-REVOLUTION

SIR – Being singularly un-enamoured of texting, twittering, and even email (except for business purposes) every time I receive an electronic communication with the postscript, "Sent from my BlackBerry Wireless Handheld" I find it hard to refrain from responding, "So what – am I supposed to be impressed?"

Robert Readman
Bournemouth, Dorset

SIR – The photograph in your newspaper of Sir Alan Sugar holding his mobile phone while looking towards the ground reminds me of many other photographs of film stars, footballers etc. who seem to have these phones welded to their hands. Are they expecting emergency calls at any moment? How did humanity survive before their invention?

It would be interesting to see from NHS records how many people have been treated in Accident and Emergency departments for walking into lampposts since mobile phones became an essential fashion accessory.

Roy Williams
Aberporth, Ceredigon

SIR – I have started writing a blog under your system and I am disappointed by the pointlessness of the comments I have received. They have nearly all been irrelevant to what I have written.

Are there any intelligent people who use this service? Apart from me, of course.

K.S.

SIR – In view of much recent political activity could one of your erudite columnists please explain what a "blog" is?

Confused
London W1

SIR – Your news website now includes noisy video commercials that blast away automatically. Rest assured, I shall not visit there again.

S.M.
The Savile Club, London W1

MODERN SPORTING STANDARDS

SIR – As Kevin Pietersen was still technically England's cricket captain when he dressed on the morning of his flight back to Britain, I take the view, having seen the photograph on the front page of the sports section, that I am glad he no longer represents me.

For any cricket captain to consider that a mode of dress inferior to my gardening attire is appropriate for someone occupying a position of national standing says much for how he respects the feelings and views of others.

And frankly, if I'd scored a seat next to anyone dressed like that for a long-haul flight I'd have asked the airline for my money back.

Standards, Kevin, standards.

Peter Harvey
Walton Highway, Norfolk

SIR – Congratulations to England on their win against the West Indies. Congratulations also to Graham Onions for his fine bowling performance. Hopefully he will remember to shave next time he appears at Lord's.

Charles James
Aldwick, West Sussex

SIR – On Saturday I finished my umpteenth reading of *Mike* and *Psmith*, P.G. Wodehouse's elegant paean to his beloved game of cricket, set in the golden years before the First World War.

Yesterday I read of proposals to play Test Matches under floodlighting, the players wearing "coloured pyjamas". I had difficulty in holding back a tear of loss and despair.

David Salter
Kew, Surrey

SIR – Forget reverse swing. Has the England team considered the tactic of reverse sledging during this Ashes series? Example: "I say, my wife tells me you're awfully good in bed."

Robert Solomon
London NW3

SIR – I have the solution to the problem whereby match officials at football games are routinely abused in various ways by the players: there should be no officials. Footballers are well known for their honesty and integrity on and off the field, so should therefore be able to police their games themselves.

A typical exchange between captains might go:
"Do you think that was a penalty, old boy?"
"Yes, old bean, you are quite correct."

Michael Johnson
Woolavington, Somerset

SIR – Am I alone in my view that Andy Murray's voice has similarities to that of Sean Connery? When his tennis days are over, will he become the new James Bond?

Bob Rattenbury
Pinner, Middlesex

SIR – Am I the only Englishman who is not bothered about which foreigner wins Wimbledon?

William Leverington
Hounslow, Middlesex

GROOMING A PAGE ONE GIRL AT ASCOT

SIR – How lovely Katherine Jenkins looked on your front page today, when she attended Ascot with her hair neatly coiled under a beautiful hat. Such a contrast to the untidy girls photographed on page three, with their long, straggly hair.

Why are so many young women today incapable of looking well groomed?

Norma Less
Great Barton, Suffolk

SIR – How lovely to see a picture of Katherine Jenkins, the most gorgeous looking woman in Britain, on your front page. I also saw her at Ascot – unfortunately not in the flesh but on television.

Her singing is also fantastic.

If you think there is a more gorgeous looking woman in Britain, can you please print her picture?

Bernard Cunningham
Hutton, Essex

SIR – I read that yesterday Katherine Jenkins "wore a deep pink dress and matching hat with giant roses". Yesterday I wore a dark blue linen jacket, khaki chinos and a blue-and-white striped shirt.

F.C.
London SW1

SIR – Looking online at your pictures of "ladies" at Aintree this week I can only thank God in His mercy for my homosexuality.

N.J.P.
Hawkhurst, Kent

SIR – Your front-page picture of Kate Winslet with a plunging neckline being up for two golden globes was most apposite.

K.J.K.

LORDS ROGERS'S BLIGHT ON THE LANDSCAPE

SIR – Following his spat with Prince Charles over Chelsea Barracks, I feel obliged to report my having seen a photograph of Lord Rogers wearing brown footwear with a dark suit.

I suspect he may also wear suede shoes in daylight hours – not the happiest of thoughts.

Derek Gibson
Cadiz, Spain

FASHION LEMMINGS IN FATAL, BUTTOCK-HUGGING DISCOMFORT

SIR – In uttering that immortal old man's phrase, "Is it just me?", am I alone in wondering what has happened to the "rise" in trousers? To the sartorially uninformed, the "rise" is the distance between the seam under the crutch and the top of the waistband. In the past, a pair of trousers, worn with or without braces and secured with a belt, would have had a waistband that sat well above the top line of the pelvic bones. Trousers with a single-pleated or double-pleated front would then hang elegantly and comfortably.

But not today. Our overseas mass manufacturers seem to think it appropriate to reduce the cost of making trousers by assuming that the human torso has no waist. The result, which some may deem fashionable, is groin- and buttock-hugging inelegance and discomfort.

On some, the shortening of the rise is fatal, exposing underwear and flesh that is most unattractive. Perhaps this is why fashion lemmings wear their shirt-tails outside their trousers?

David Culm
Littleover, Derbyshire

SIR – Never mind the expenses scandal, I wish to expose another very worrying development.

I recently purchased a pack of underpants from Marks & Spencer, only to discover that they had replaced the flap label with an imprint which is unreadable in the half light. Getting them on the right way round when I dress is therefore a lottery. Putting the light on is not an option.

I tried phoning Marks & Spencer to complain but wasn't understood as I now speak with a squeaky voice.

Graham Adams
Brightlingsea, Essex

SIR – One of the better moments of supermarket shopping is being offered, at the checkout, "a wine carrier". I can't help but imagine a person attired in elegantly draped robes, perhaps holding an amphora with some fat glistening grapes . . . only for my reverie to be interrupted by the presentation of a rather inelegant but highly efficient self-assembly cardboard contraption.

Barbara Beattie
Neston, Cheshire

SIR – A tip for your readers to avoid delay: Never stand behind Satan in a Post Office queue as the Devil takes many forms.

Courtenay Young
London SW5

GIVE US SOME CREDIT

SIR – The modern bank statement appears to be designed to encompass the lowest common denominator. Most banks now employ the terms "Money out" and "Money in" in place of "Debit" and "Credit".

Am I right to be insulted by this, or is it simply the case that educational standards are now so abysmal that the modern pupil and/or employee simply cannot understand these terms?

I am tempted to say "Give us some credit", but that is probably asking too much of a bank.

Keith Haines
Belfast

D-DAY REWRITTEN

SIR – Judging from book reviews and press and television coverage of the 65th anniversary of the Normandy landings, am I alone in thinking it was purely an American/German affair?

Terence Edgar
Wallasey, Wirral

EU STEALS OUR SWEETS

SIR – In the midst of all this doom and gloom I hesitate to offer more disturbing news, but I must warn readers that both Barretts and Tesco have seen fit to remove the all-important sherbet centre from sherbet sweets.

Is there no end to the destruction of those things we hold so dear?

Please do not tell me that the EU is to blame. Not that I would be surprised.

G.A.B.

SIR – I never thought I would say this, but I feel rather envious of the Iraqis. They are celebrating "Sovereignty Day" – the day on which American forces leave their country and allow them to manage their own affairs.

I look forward to the day when we in Britain can celebrate the return of our sovereignty – the day when we finally manage to extricate ourselves from the political tyranny of the European Union.

Ian Johnson
Chelford, Cheshire

CRY GOD FOR STILTON CHEESE

SIR – The picture on the front page of your paper yesterday filled me with pride. Her Majesty, the Queen, our Armed Forces and Big Ben are the few vestiges of worth which Europe and the politicians have left us, especially those who can remember the time when this country possessed an identity.

Once more unto the breach, dear friends! Cry God for Stilton cheese, Morris dancing and Enid Blyton!

Mrs C. Judd
Romsey, Hampshire

IMMORTALISING THE WINDSORS

SIR –

I am assured that I will not
be the next poet laureate,
not summonsed by the Windsors who
think immortality their due,
treat every anniversary,
each birthday, gala, garden tea,
with royal respect. I'd cause offence
with levity, indifference,
the constant dread her Majesty
might die expecting verse from me;
concerned that loosed, my random styles
would not tease tears, but tickle smiles.
I need not fear, sure for my part
safe anonymity. To start,
I'm not in print or known at all;
would be flattered to get a call
from HMQ, offering me
a laurel crown, fine wine for free.
Those I'll leave to all in the eye
of fame and fortune; so that I
can quietly wield my blunt 2B,
and scribble libel privately.

Patricia Eade
Winchester

SIR –
Her Majesty The Queen
May or may not be the merriest monarch we've ever seen.
But she's a lot less sinister
Than the Prime Minister.

Yours awaiting office,
Peter Wyton
Longlevens, Gloucestershire

SIR – When I read that Edward Stourton's future with the BBC was in question, it was in the context of an offensive remark he had made about the Queen Mother.

If this is indeed true he should, in my opinion, lose his head and not just his job.

Rhona Mogridge
Henley on Thames, Oxfordshire

THE PRINCE OF BRACKNELL BUS STATION

SIR – Now that Prince Charles is entitled to a free bus pass I do hope that he does not bring too many minders with him when he travels on the 195 from Great Hollands to Bracknell Bus station. It sometimes get rather crowded.

Rev Michael Bentley
Bracknell, Berkshire

THE PRINCES OF POLITICAL CORRECTNESS

SIR – I feel very sorry that Lt Harry Wales has been forced to make a public apology for an apparent racist remark made in the privacy of his small team of Sandhurst cadets.

I served in the army in the 1950s, and as an officer in the Territorial Army for 30 subsequent years. I commanded "Taffy" Williams, "Paddy" Barriscale, "Jock" Sinclair, "Scouse" Gelsthorpe, and "Geordie" Holland, and no doubt if I had commanded a black soldier, he would have been "Sambo" or "Golly", a Chinese would have been "Chinky", and an Asian, "Packy". I have no intention of issuing an apology to any of these former comrades.

In my office in London in the early 1970s I worked with a very lovely coloured lady whom we nicknamed "Chocolate Drop". She thought it highly amusing and was not at all offended.

We really are taking political correctness too far.

Michael Clemson
Horsmonden, Kent

SIR – I am getting more and more exasperated by endless political correctness. If Prince Charles wants to call his friend Sooty, Fatty, Ginger, Loony, Owl (of the Remove), or anything else, and the friend does not object, what business is it of anyone else? This is just another example of meddling by people with nothing better to do than find fault with others.

I am (more and more) "Disgusted of Tunbridge Wells".

Mrs S.M.L. Cary
Gravesend, Kent

SIR – When I played against Harrow in the 1950s, there were, as far as I recall, two "Sooties" and a "Darkie", all very good chaps. The trouble with the PC brigade is that they cannot get to grips with British humour, and take themselves too seriously.

I.P.F. Meiklejohn
Blervie, Moray

SIR – In defence of Prince Harry I have to say that after 30 years residency in this country, I trust people a lot more who call me a "f***** German bastard" to my face than those who hide their prejudices behind a veneer of discreet bourgeois politeness.

Reiner Luyken
Achiltibuie, Ross-shire

SIR – Two minor race row allegations against our royal Princes are two too many. Neither was considered offensive by the majority of those canvassed, nor, clearly, was "Sooty" upset in any way whatsoever.

I served in Devonshire from 1964 until 1966. We had two coloured sailors in our ship's company. They were known by everybody from the Captain downwards as "Midnight" (the darker) and "23:59" (the lighter). Both revelled in their titles and were respected as first-class sailors.

Cdr M.R. RN (Retd)
Bath

SIR – An African-type gentleman walked into our pub today and asked for a pint of "Nigerian lager". We looked at him in bewilderment; he then pointed to the Guinness pump and repeated his request. We fell about laughing and our barman jumped to the gentleman's request.

Where we do we go from here?

Mike Fowler
Chilmark, Wiltshire

ONE NATION, UNDER MANY GODS

SIR – Now that the *Telegraph* has championed calls for Hindu funeral pyres in the English countryside, may I commission your support for my own preferred burial arrangements? As a member of the little-known Arboreal faith, I wish my remains to be placed in the branches of a large tree. Perhaps discreet areas in municipal parks could be set aside to accommodate the faithful.

A. Lester
Stanley Pontlarge, Gloucestershire

RICHARD DAWKINS'S ROAD TO DAMASCUS

SIR – Some years ago now a young chap called Saul was on his way to Damascus with every intention of persecuting Christians. Suddenly, there was a blinding flash and Jesus spoke to him. After three days of prayer and fasting, Saul became one of the strongest advocates for Christ there has ever been. Richard Dawkins should therefore be ready: God might decide to use some of that evangelistic zeal on him.

S.W.
Ipswich, Suffolk

SIR – Looking at your picture of Charles Darwin led me to speculate about the evolutionary purpose of a bald head and bushy beard. Does anyone know?

D.M.
Manchester

LADY MADONNA, CHILDREN AT HER FEET

SIR – When Madonna moved to England she said she wanted to feel more English.

She is shortly to become a single mother with three children from different fathers. Job done, then.

H.B.
Arkley, Hertfordshire

MARVELLOUS MARMALADE

SIR – For many years I have been wondering why the shape of my piece of toast and marmalade invariably looks like a map of England when I am halfway through eating it.

Perhaps it indicates the intense Englishness of the debate about marmalade on your Letters page recently. It certainly underlines the fact that there can be no other country in the world capable of maintaining such a long-running national debate about a breakfast preserve.

J.P.
Harrogate, North Yorkshire

CORNERS
OF FOREIGN
FIELDS

THE WARM WAR

SIR – Am I alone in thinking we should tell Vladimir Putin to stick his gas-pipe up his fundament and apply a lighted match to it?

M.E. Martin
Southborough, Kent

O'BAMANIA

SIR – If the American Democratic candidate wanted to court the Irish-American vote, would he consider changing his name to Barack O'Bama?

P.K.

SIR – Let me give you a little advice: stay out of our business here in the USA. You have no right to comment, critique or even nod towards us. It is against OUR laws for any foreign power to try and affect our elections. You are meddling.

Now, you can hate us, hate our country and our President. You can abuse John McCain and Sarah Palin all you and your stuck-up British prissyness want to, but the fact remains that the election is close; Mac is not backing down. In fact, I know for sure he and Ms Sarah are going to beat the little Messiah and his snooty Gaf master Joe Biden like red-haired stepchildren.

But hey, have fun living with Sharia Law – that's what your Eurotrash white guilt gives you.

Anon
New York, USA

SIR – Your paper is very liberal. Of course, what can you expect from a socialist, faggot country like England?

I am proud to be from the best country in the world: the USA! And from the best state in the USA: Texas!

Bring your socialist, gay-loving ass to Texas and we will kick your ass.

Oh, and we are allowed to carry handguns here. In fag countries like yours even the "bobbies" can't have guns.

M.L.
Texas, USA

A PRESIDENT WHO CAMPAIGNED IN POETRY....

SIR –

There's a black man living in the White House,
Now what d'ya think of that?
I don't give a Dickens
So long as he's a Democrat.
So long as he cracks the credit crunch,
Bringing wealth to all mankind.
So long as he gets us peace on earth
By Friday dinner time.
So long as he makes the planet green,
Is all things to all men on earth,
I don't care about the colour of his skin
Nor his place of birth.
What did you say his name was?
Jesus Christ, our Saviour?
No, he has a Muslim name:
Barack Hussein Obama.

Avril Jessey
Cobham, Surrey

... AND GOVERNED IN PROSE

SIR – I am not surprised that President Obama is having difficulties. Oratory isn't everything. I've taken to calling him the Hawaiian Windbag.

Cuillin Scott
Edinburgh

SIR – I am proud to announce that I did not watch the in-awe-guration of President Obama. I don't need him, I am my own man.

Doug Harris
Stockton-on-Tees

SIR – President Obama's acolytes laud his more "humane" approach to the world while ridiculing George W. Bush's diplomatic record. Yet George got the North Koreans to the negotiating table four times. What do Obama's marshmallow meanderings get him? A very long range rocket right up the bum! Ohwhattabumma!

H.H.
Victoria, Australia

SIR – My sincerest apology for the Bungler-in-Chief that some stupid Americans voted into office. What were they thinking? Barack Obama and his wife have no class and have treated Britain in a most terrible manner by snubbing Gordon Brown on his visit. It seems a silk purse cannot be made out of a sow's ear.

Again, he and his wife do not represent all of America – they only represent the welfare queens and the liberals who are ruining our country.

Please pray for us.

Emilie
USA

SIR – Should Gordon Brown show a lack of imagination and reciprocate the DVD gift supplied by Barack Obama, I do hope and pray that he does not leave the selection in the hands of Jacqui Smith.

Stephen Phoenix
Harpenden, Hertfordshire

PLEASE FORWARD TO THE WHITE HOUSE

SIR – IS IT POSSIBLE YOU COULD FORWARD THE LETTER I SENT YOU TO PRESIDENT OBAMA AS YOU ARE IN A BETTER POSITION TO DO SO?

I AM NOT GOOD WITH COMPUTERS!

IT MAY REMOTELY HELP HIM!
THANKS!

T.C.

SIR – May I advise Barack Obama through your publication that I will not be prepared to serve in his administration. The same applies to Gordon Brown and David Cameron.

Justin Pryor
Beckenham, Kent

PWOTECTING THE PWESIDENT

SIR – I see that the Secret Service codenames for Barack Obama and his family have been announced. Mr Obama is called Renegade, while his wife Michelle is Renaissance and their daughters Rosebud and Radiance.

The names are chosen to be easily pronounced and understood when agents use radio communications. Jonathan Ross had better not apply for a job in the Presidential detail.

Steve Cattell
Hougham, Lincolnshire

SIR – I believe that Barack Obama and Jonathan Ross are both 47 years old. There the similarity ends.

Colin Stone
Cellardyke, Fife

SIR – The following takes place between November 4 2008 and November 4 2012. Events take place in real time. Obama's first action: appoint Jack Bauer as head of security.

T.P.

SIR – For his own protection, will the new American President now be surrounded by Barack-Aides?

Colin Allen
London N20

L'ENTENTE NOT SO CORDIALE

SIR – In whose deranged mind can it be a good idea for the French government to own our present and future nuclear power generation? This is a vital strategic resource for Britain and should in no circumstances be owned by a foreign power, especially the French.

Richard Tonge
Keig, Aberdeenshire

SIR – Can you imagine watching the French Open at Roland Garros with all the players drinking British mineral water? The French would go on strike straight away.

However, the Wimbledon authorities have seen fit to provide bottles of French mineral water for the players – this despite British businesses struggling to survive the worst recession in living memory. How's that for another own goal?

Al Ellis
West Kirby, Wirral

SIR – The fact that Nicolas Sarkozy, Gordon Brown and the Duke of Edinburgh were just bit players when Carla Bruni visited Britain simply proves that women – particularly elegant, beautiful women – hold the real power these days. How misguided they would be to try to emulate us pathetic and feeble-minded men.

Brian Christley
Abergele, Conwy

SIR – Could it be said that Sarkozm is the lowest form of twit?

John Thewlis
London SE1

FRENCH GLOBAL TIME

SIR – Why don't we make 2012 the first year of the new order? I propose that on January 1, we start with months of either 28 or 35 days, adding up to 385 for every year. No more leap years, no more leap seconds and incidentally no more time zones.

The French people would have the privilege of starting the 12-hour countdown to the new time system at midday on December 31 2011. I know that the new order of one artificial time for the world means that opening times for shops etc. that do not run 24/7 will have to be negotiated, but this is world harmony we are talking about.

I certainly would be happy to reset my alarm clock rather than go through the bother of British Summer Time.

Mike Jordan
Worcester

NO FOREIGN LANGUAGES PLEASE, WE'RE BRITISH

SIR – Are examination boards going to offer a qualification in shouting loudly in English in order to compensate for the poor take-up of modern languages at GCSE? Many children and adults would easily pass this test.

Catherine Stanley
Hale, Cheshire

WESTMINSTER'S
VILLAGE
IDIOTS

HOME MOVIES

SIR – Am I alone in being dismayed by the greater level of concern being expressed about Jacqui Smith's misappropriation of a trivial amount of public money for private entertainment than that we have a Home Secretary whose husband watches pornographic movies?

David Salter
Kew, Surrey

SIR – Jacqui and Jacquoff?

B.W.

SIR – Jacqui Smith's husband has my sympathy. A chap has to find something to do if his wife is always away at her sister's.

Brian Sheridan
Sheffield

SIR – Which movies were they?
Trussed no-one, featuring Gordon Brown?
Is that a financial black hole? with Alistair Darling?
Quantitative Sleazing?

Roger Sinden
Mansel Lacy, Herefordshire

SIR – I see that one of the so-called pornographic films viewed by Jacqui Smith's husband bore the rivetingly descriptive title *Raw Meat*. Therein lies the man's error. Instead of sending the bill to the Home Office for settlement, he should have sent it to Defra.

Eric Jones
Southport

SIR – They still criticise poor old Nero for fiddling while Rome burned. At least he wasn't watching pornographic movies.

M.R. Scott
Co Kerry, Ireland

SIR – Surely this porn in a teacup with the Home Secretary has peaked and will blow over soon?

Lawrence Fraser
Elgin, Moray

MUGGED BY PLANET WESTMINSTER

SIR – Am I the only one who feels he has been repeatedly mugged by a bunch of serial-muggers from Planet Westminster?

Ferri Jahed
New Ash Green, Kent

SIR – Isn't it amazing how all those MPs who entered Parliament to help the poor and underprivileged made sure they got their noses in the trough first? They wonder why nobody bothers to vote. All 647 of them put together aren't worth a cup of cold p***.

Martin Armstrong
Tunbridge Wells, Kent

SIR – *The Daily Telegraph* is quite right to have published details of MPs' abuse of the expenses system. Britain is currently run by a bunch of self-deluding, mendacious onanists.

A.B. (ex-pat who moved away in anticipation of the current situation)
Co. Donegal, Ireland

SIR – *The Daily Telegraph* is to be commended for its exposé of MPs' expenses but it should also be saluted for its bravery. I confidently expect to read shortly that the Government has ordered your offices to be raided by the Security Forces (without the knowledge of the Prime Minister), your computers removed and your editor detained under anti-terrorism legislation and threatened with life imprisonment.

If it is any consolation, I will be happy, should such an event occur, to send your editor a food parcel and some underwater breathing equipment.

Gerald Payman
Tenbury Wells, Worcestershire

SIR – In celebration of the 500th anniversary of Henry VIII, would it not be appropriate for taxpayers to fund a scaffold at the Palace of Westminster and deal with the hung, drawn and quartered?

C.A.

SIR – May I point out that MPs should be entitled to a fair hearing, then they should all be shot.

Sheila Shaw
Nelson, Lancashire

SIR – Last week I happened upon our local MP Bill Cash. Incensed by recent revelations, I approached him and the conversation went like this:
Me: I've always voted for you.
BC: Thank you
Me: However, I won't be voting for you any more.
BC: Oh.
Me: I don't know how you have the brass neck to show your face around here.
BC: I don't think you know all the details.
Me: Oh yes I do, I read the *Telegraph*.
Exit stage left.
Thanks to you, I have found my voice.

Patricia Skelton
Swynnerton, Staffordshire

SIR – Your recent revelations indicate how many MPs own inordinately large houses. This shows that we are either ruled by Old Money or by the Nouveau Riche who have enriched themselves at the taxpayers' expense. Neither alternative is especially heart-warming.

Richard Hathway
Evesham, Worcestershire

SIR – Now we know why they are called "Members".
Could anyone please explain "honourable"?

Richard Lines
Modbury, Devon

SIR – Am I the only one struck by the similarity
between the "only obeying the rules" defence,
proffered by some members of today's House of
Commons, and the infamous "only obeying orders"
mitigation attempted at Nuremberg after the end of
the Second World War?

Frank Wilson
Huddersfield, West Yorkshire

SIR – Your publication of MPs' expenses has given us
a glimpse of what it will be like at the end of the
world, on the Day of Judgment.

You have exposed claims that the MPs thought, or
hoped, would remain private. Each of us makes
moral decisions that we hope will remain hidden.
But the Bible speaks of a day when the books will be
opened before God and all mankind, and each
person judged accordingly.

A.M.
St Albans, Hertfordshire

SIR – Is the *Telegraph* guilty of its own expenses cover-up story? It is very hard to believe that there are no claims for massages, ladies of the night or previously unknown gender reassignment. Or is it a case of "watch this space"?

Julie La Coste
Lamberhurst, Kent

SIR – At school I always laughed at the way Latin verbs were declined – quite regularly apart from the first person plural and third person plural.
Might I suggest:

I redact
You redact
He redacted
We redactedissimus
You redacted
They stuffed us

Robert Smith
Brentford, Middlesex

SIR – I have been trying to cancel my Setanta subscription with no success. Can you help? It would make a nice change from MPs' expenses.

E. Luders
Knebworth, Hertfordshire

SIR – Am I alone in worrying what really bad news has been buried in the last three weeks?

Enid Pillidge
Woking, Surrey

SIR – Am I alone in now being thoroughly bored by the MPs' expenses business?

Jeremy Parr
Suckley, Worcestershire

SIR – I'm sure I'm not alone in looking forward to your investigation of the expenses system at the House of Lords.

Sue Bright
Twickenham, Middlesex

AYO JOANNA

SIR – The only person I can think of with a clean bill of health to vote for in the next general election is Joanna Lumley.

That's even though she has a tendency to drink expensive champagne and shout "Ayo Gurkhali", which translates, I believe, as "Up Yours".

R. Peacock
Woodley, Berkshire

IF YOU'RE UNHAPPY AND YOU KNOW IT

SIR – I have pleasure in sending you one of my little ditties, sung to a well-known tune, which may be appreciated by other taxpayers:

If you want a big TV, never mind.
You can get it all for free, so never mind.
If you crave an antique hearth
Or gold fittings on your bath
Just claim it on expenses
And never mind!

If you'd like a second home, never mind.
Or a holiday in Rome, never mind.
You can rob taxpayers blind,
Fiddling all that you can find,
Your expense sheets will be signed,
So, never mind!

If you fancy hiring porn, never mind.
You can watch from dusk till dawn, never mind.
Should your garden need new fences,
Why not claim it on expenses?
You're an MP now, my friend,
So, never mind!

An MP's life is hard, but never mind.
You can use your credit card, so never mind.

Hire a limousine for work,
Just one more little perk,
Slap it down on your expense sheet,
And NEVER MIND!

Maurice Daines
Bembridge, Isle of Wight

SIR – In light of your newspaper's revelations, it would seem timely to reconsider Arthur Benson's words "Land of Hope and Glory" which are sung to Edward Elgar's *Pomp and Circumstance March*. I offer the following parody:

Land of Labour and Tory, what can we claim for free?
How shall we defraud thee, who are paid by thee?
Wider still and wider shall expenses be met;
You who made me an MP, make me wealthier yet.
You who made me an MP, make me wealthier yet.

Dr Peter D. Clarkson
Cambridge

SIR – Well done for exposing that hornets' nest of MPs' expenses. I have written my thoughts in verse (this often happens when a stimulating subject comes up):

What a shambles, what a shower,
Those oh so noble folk in power.
Neighing, braying, puffed-up fools,
Who spend our money (within the rules)
On porn, on lightbulbs, kitchen sinks,
Dog food, Tampax, crisps, soft drinks,
Private transport, and bills for 'phones,
We even buy them second homes.
Our ever-open public purse is
Not for teachers, nor for nurses.
Cleaners count, designers too,
But for MPs, not me or you.
Reserved for spivs in tie and jacket,
Who steal our money, what a racket!
Parliament's now lined with sleaze.
Right Honourable Members, the House of Thieves.

Jackie Grearson
Bournemouth

SIR – On first looking into ministers' expenses (with apologies to Keats)

Much has been rumour'd of the realms of gold
In which dwell politicians, yet unsaid.
But now we hear of Nutty's featherbed
And Prescott's bogseat, hope it's not too cold.
"Come clean!" we cry, yet we know Brown of old.
His jaw aslack as if he is half dead,
He's drawling some irrelevance instead.
Seems terrified lest truth should e'er be told.
Then felt I like a watcher of Star Trek
When Klingons or some other alien
Outsmart us with their greed and sheer brass neck.
So otherworldly seems this race of men
And women, funded by the taxpayer's cheque
While sitting on their bums in Number Ten.

    A.C.

SPEAKING THE SPEAKER'S LANGUAGE

SIR – Michael Martin's inability to do his job brings to mind a comment made by the First Mate of a ship in which I served to a Glaswegian sailor at the helm: "Son, you could not steer a turd round a p*** pot with a walking stick."

It is a language I am sure that the former Speaker would understand.

M.C.
Disley, Cheshire

SIR – In the days of yore a man of the Speaker's behaviour would have been debagged by his peers and thrown into the nearest horse trough.

Ian Macdonald
Butleigh, Somerset

SIR – Am I alone in finding the current process of choosing a Speaker at best unseemly and at worst thoroughly damaging to the dignity of the office?

The present system of Members setting out their stalls like job-seekers in a medieval hiring-fare does nothing for the prestige of Parliament.

Leonard Allen
Marham, Norfolk

SIR – I find it difficult to take John Bercow, the new Speaker, seriously. When he sits in his huge seat, my mind is filled with the image of Ronnie Corbett telling stories on *The Two Ronnies*.

Barry Furness
Fareham, Hampshire

SIR – What a pity that Parliament did not wait until Wimbledon to elect a new Speaker. The umpires there, both male and female, have infinitely more gravitas, authority, impartiality and control over their charges. They are also far better dressed.

Robie Uniacke
Easebourne, West Sussex

FANTASY CABINET

SIR – Fantasy football and fantasy cricket provide amusement for many. But on a more serious note relating to getting us out of the current mess I suggest the following cross-party "Fantasy Cabinet" to supply the necessary brains, experience, charisma, and common sense necessary for the task ahead: William Hague, Sir "Eddie" George, Simon Heffer, John Redwood, Boris Johnson, David Davis, Christopher Booker, Sir Bernard Ingham, Iain Duncan Smith and Theodore Dalrymple.

Catherine Timms
Edinburgh

SIR – It is a national tragedy that the likes of Simon Heffer, Iain Martin and Jeff Randall do not have access to the levers of power.

Nigel Thompson
Wellingborough, Northamptonshire

SIR – The answer to Gordon Brown's problems surely lie in offering Margaret Thatcher an important job in his newly reshuffled Cabinet.

Do you think that he could be suitably perspicacious to give it a try? After all, he has nothing to lose and everything to gain.

J.A. Jee
Manchester

A TAXI DRIVER AND I

SIR – During a long taxi journey the driver, in his sixties, and I talked about a number of issues on which we both agreed:
1. Prisoners set free after completing half their sentence. This is a disgrace.
2. Human Rights Act. A heaven-sent piece of legislation for slick lawyers, bogus asylum seekers, terrorists and crooks and villains in general.
3. Benefits. The Labour Party has created a society of people reliant on handouts – and why not, if these same people vote for you?

4. Unmarried young mothers. No wonder there is such an upsurge.

5. Immigration. In some areas the very fabric of society is breaking down as hordes of immigrants flood in.

Any political party that can tackle these issues would probably get the vote of 75 per cent of the electorate – is there anyone out there listening?

P.T. Costello
Newcastle upon Tyne

SIR – Recently you published the results of a survey that showed taxi drivers to be the rudest people we are likely to encounter in daily life.

Last week on a visit to London, which happened to clash with the tube strike, I decided to check this out. I took six cab rides and found that on the whole the drivers were polite, helpful and extremely patient.

However, one thing I noticed was that the affability of the driver seemed to be in direct proportion to his head of hair. The most chatty and ebullient driver had a profuse mop, while the one with little to say, apart from cursing at the cyclists, was clean-shaven.

Is there a clue here somewhere to judging human behaviour?

B.A. Maskell
Croyde, Devon

HELLO DARKNESS, OUR OLD FRIEND

SIR – Am I alone in cringing every time I hear the four words "Lord Mandelson, Business Secretary" in conjunction?

Peter Senneck
Churchdown, Gloucestershire

SIR – Who'd have thought it? Lord Mandelson (why do our fingers tremble so when his name is prefixed with such an honorific?) is now touted as a potential Brutus to deliver the tap on the shoulder to Gordon Brown to let him know his time is up.

At least it's nice to know that in a time of constant change, the queen can still be a kingmaker.

J.A.
Torquay, Devon

SIR – It would appear that the unelected and unelectable Lord Meddlesome is now running the country. Just when are we, the British Public, going to take to the streets and demand a general election. We need a leader – *The Daily Telegraph* maybe?

Stuart Kempster
Albaston, Cornwall

SIR – Is Mandelson getting covered in green custard
the first known case of the flan hitting the s***?

Kim Thonger
Olney, Buckinghamshire

SIR – We expect our Tories to be greedy, our
nationalists to have massive chips on both shoulders
and a bleeding-heart liberal to have a conscience.
But a champagne-quaffing, foie gras-scoffing ****
with a hastily made-up lordship, masquerading as a
socialist is completely unpalatable. Who does he have
pictures of? We should be told.

Lawrence Fraser
Elgin, Moray

PS I presume **** will be edited in the unlikely event
of this being published. May I suggest "stick insect"
as an alternative?

SIR –
So 'you' put him in charge of 'UK Big Business'.
And let him 'deal' with 'Jaguar Land Rover'.
ONLY IN BRITAIN.
Would they put 'The Fox'.
In charge of 'The Hen House'!
cc 'MI5'
'The City'
'UK Big Business'

M

WHO DOES NICK GRIFFIN
THINK HE HIS?

SIR – Am I the only one to have noticed that Nick Griffin, the leader of the BNP, hardly appears to mirror the fair-haired, Anglo Saxon type that he and his party appear to wish to support?

Perhaps he ought to have his racial background checked by the BBC's *Who do you think you are?* team. If it transpired that his ancestors were not the blond giants of mythical Aryan legend buried beneath the Greenland ice cap he could then arrange to do the decent thing: deport himself and leave the rest of us in peace.

Ted Shorter
Hildenborough, Kent

IS YOUR MP A CHRISTIAN?

SIR – I can tell by someone's eyes whether they are a genuine Christian or not. This has generally enabled me to discuss subjects such as homosexuality and hell without fear of suspension, dismissal or even arrest, like some Gospel preachers have been subject to.

I recommend you visit your MP, smile at them and if their eyes don't light up, he or she is unlikely to be a Christian.

R.D.
London N1

TONY BLAIR AND THE HOUND OF HISTORY

SIR – I was surprised by your article in which Cherie Blair predicted that history will judge Tony Blair as a significant world figure and that "he'll be up there with Churchill".

Is it likely that she means the dog in the insurance advertisement? Oh yes!

Tim Rann
Mirfield, West Yorkshire

SIR – Should it ever be decided to reprint the photograph of a coquettish Cherie Blair gazing wide-eyed through her eyelashes, will you be good enough to issue a health warning on the first page? I'm sure my heart rate more than doubled at this horrendous sight first thing in the morning and it is an experience I'd be happy to forgo in future.

Personally, I have no interest in the haverings of a woman who has proved herself to be no more than an educated idiot.

George Wilkie
Hemingford Grey, Cambridgeshire

SIR – I feel I really must write to thank you for the picture you published of Cherie Blair. I cut it out, laminated it and pinned it to my shed door. Without any sort of locking device, my shed has been absolutely safe from thieves and vandals.

Peter Osborne
Skelton-in-Cleveland, North Yorkshire

BROWN'S BOOM AND BOAST

SIR – I wish Gordon Brown were not so boastful. He boasts all the time. It's bad manners, and very off-putting.

He also booms at us more than is agreeable.

I'm quite looking forward to no more Boom and Boast.

Nicholas Guitard
Poundstock, Cornwall

SIR – I might be alone in feeling like I do but I must say that the flat, dull, monotonous sound of Gordon Brown's voice sends my spirits into steep freefall. The fact that he seems completely detached from reality generates fear but it is not as bad as the pain of listening to the sound of his voice.

Mick Ferrie
Mawnan Smith, Cornwall

SIR – I recall a novelty single from my youth entitled *Gordon is a moron*. Is it not time for its re-release?

D.W.
St Peter Port, Guernsey

SIR – Having failed, to date, to promote the engagement of Prince William to Kate Middleton in order to divert public attention from his political troubles, did anyone notice Gordon Brown personally giving a dead-leg to Rafael Nadal in a similarly motivated attempt to help Andy Murray's chances at Wimbledon?

Graham Hoyle
Baildon, West Yorkshire

SIR – I don't see the problem with Jeremy Clarkson's remarks about the Prime Minister. Gordon Brown *is* Scottish, he *does* have only one eye and he *is* an idiot. Is a man to be chastised now for telling the truth?

Andrea Hunt
Datchet, Berkshire

SIR – I do wish you would stop referring to Gordon Brown as the Prime Minister and employ the more appropriate appellation "sub-prime minister" instead.

For many years I have described him as "Brezhnev Brown" and week by week the similarities become more marked. To name but three (ignoring the obvious physical similarity): they were both unelected, both completely unconnected with reality and both presided over the demise of their respective regimes.

David Sherman
London N3

SIR – On reading your headline "Brown losing his bounce over the economic crisis", my husband's comment was: "Brown is a spin bowler. How could he ever achieve bounce at his pace?"

Wendy G. Perkins
Lyminge, Kent

SIR – Global warming gets blamed for everything nowadays. Could it be blamed for Gordon Brown?

Christine Jones
Treddol, Denbighshire

SIR – May I advise the bearers of the surname Brown, for the sake of their male descendants yet to come, that they eschew the forename Gordon for a few thousand years – or at least until the combination is no longer synonymous with "prat".

George Brown
St Jean d'Angely, France

SIR – Recently a member of the Cabinet said that Gordon Brown should be allowed to get on and deal with the real issues. I would suggest that he should be selling the *Big Issue*, preferably in Scotland.

Jack Major (No relation)
Budleigh Salterton, Devon

SIR – This morning my wife and I were discussing the current Labour Party situation with particular relevance to Gordon Brown. She remarked to me that he was "as safe as houses". I think she may be right.

R. Milnthorpe
Emsworth, West Sussex

SIR – I'm hopping mad. I've had enough. Come on you *Telegraph* chaps let's get out and rally. My placard is ready: BROWN OUT

Stanley Medicks
London N3

SIR – I got very excited when I read the headline: "I made one last effort but now it's time to go". It was only when I realised that the article referred to the cricketer Michael Vaughan that my euphoria turned to despair.

David Packer
Pembury, Kent

SIR – Might all Gordon Brown's problems be solved were he to start wearing lipstick? Or would he still be Gordon Brown?

Kim Thonger
Olney, Buckinghamshire

SIR – It appears that the only two things that this useless Government has pulled off are its ability to do U-turns and its propensity for having makeovers. Is this the first Government in history where the men wear more make-up than the women?

K.H.

SIR – Your front page supposedly shows Gordon Brown spontaneously kissing his wife. Am I the only one to notice that he is not giving her a proper kiss at all? He is pretending by giving a stage kiss – on the chin.

Nigel Lawrence
Nottingham

SIR – I read your report, "Prime Minister Gordon Brown drowning in bankers", and I disagree. I have seen his videos about the G20 plan in London, improving the economy, banking system, employment etc.

I will always be at his side, because I will marry him soon.

Thank you so much for letting me speak about this; I hope we can keep in touch.

Love always!

Susan Gordon Brown

SIR – As Wendy Cope does not seem to want the job of Poet Laureate, I would like to be considered. This is one of my more recent works:

Gordon is a naughty boy, he's been bad all his life,
He's buggered up the country now,
Despite his lovely wife.

Do you think I may be in with a chance?

Lesley Williams
Slough, Berkshire

SIR – Gordon Brown has now admitted, in the *Guardian*, that he could walk away. Unfortunately, we can't walk away from him. In anticipation of that happy day when he finally does retire (which can't be long now) I have written the following poem.

> *You, more than your peers,*
> *Have wrecked the past 12 years,*
> *Realised our worst fears,*
> *So spare us false tears*
> *And the Hazel Blears,*
> *Just say Goodbye. Cheers.*

John Salkeld
London SE22

SIR –

> *Smiley little Hazel Blears,*
> *Isn't she a cutie?*
> *If she's knifing Gordon Brown,*
> *Maybe it's her duty.*

Iain McDonald
Johnstone, Renfrewshire

SIR –

The curfew tolls the knell of parting day,
The lowing Members wind slowly o'er the lea,
The Prime Minister homeward plods his weary way,
And leaves us all in darkness; you and me.

Now fades the glimmering landscape on that sight,
And all Parliament a solemn stillness holds,
Save where the Speaker does now take his flight,
And languid murmurings lull the distant fold.

Bertram Jerrard
Fordingbridge, Hampshire

ED BALLS'S DOUBLE ACT

SIR – Whenever I see Gordon Brown and Ed Balls, the Education Secretary, together I cannot help being reminded of Mr Grimsdale and Norman Wisdom in those 1950s' British comedies.

If only the former were as innocuous as the latter.

Tony Paget
Silsden, West Yorkshire

SIR – It seems the Education Secretary is between a rock and a hard place in the debate over the future of Sats. Given his name, this is not a good place for him to be.

Pam Chadwick
Lechlade, Gloucestershire

DAVID AND GOLIATH

SIR – Have any other readers noticed the uncanny resemblance the actor in the current advertisement for the Inland Revenue self-assessment tax reminder has to David Miliband, the Foreign Secretary?

The advertisement shows the man to be a complete geek who cannot even ask a colleague for a date with any degree of confidence. Is this accidental or does someone in the advertising agency have Conservative tendencies? Is it a wicked conspiracy to damage the hapless boy David?

L.K.
Rayleigh, Essex

SIR – Can I suggest a new verb for the English language? To Miliband – meaning to be photographed with your eyes shut and a silly expression on your face.

Nigel Lawrence
Nottingham

HARRY POTTER AND THE SOCIALIST TARTAN ARMY

SIR – I see that J.K. Rowling has donated £1million to the Labour Party. Now we all know that Harry Potter is probably gay but does this mean that he is a young socialist as well? Is Hogwarts actually the headquarters of the Scottish Tartan Army Socialist Institution – or Stasi for short?

Iain MacQueen-Sims
Wargrave, Berkshire

SIR – Baroness Rowling would make a very attractive addition to the Chamber. I can just imagine her, cosily wrapped in ermine, with their lordships grouped around her, hugging their knees on the red benches while she tells them scary stories.

Don Anderson
London SW19

BLONDES OF A FEATHER

SIR – I have been convinced for many years that the political gaffe stakes have, regrettably, been held by the Conservative party. However, I am also convinced that Carol Thatcher and Boris Johnson are one and the same person: hair, intellect, gaffe-factor – you name it.

The similarity is quite frightening. Has anyone ever seen them together (pictures, please)?

C.H.P. Piff
Downley, Buckinghamshire

FAMILY LIFE
AND
TRIBULATIONS

VICIOUS VACUUMS

SIR – The most annoying thing in my life at present is the cord in my vacuum cleaner which suddenly winds itself back into the machine with no help.

Am I alone with this problem?

I.G. Anderson
Merriott, Somerset

MY WIFE AND I

SIR – My wife has banned me from moaning about the weather in her hearing. Am I alone in facing such a draconian imposition?

Tim Butler
Baulking Green, Oxfordshire

SIR – Sir Alan Sugar maintains that making money is better than sex. He obviously has not slept with my wife.

Michael West
Eastleigh, Hampshire

SIR – I read with humour the advertisements on buses stating that there may not be a God. Obviously these people have not met my wife.

Roy Stainton
Poole, Dorset

SIR – I read with interest the new idea that one way to tell when a woman is most fertile is that the tone of her voice goes up. The only drawback is that women's voices do the same thing when they're angry (and I should know).

I can only conclude that this is a potentially life-threatening way of trying to have a baby. Read the signs wrong and she might just end up beating you to death instead.

Phil Bailey
Crickhowell, Powys

SIR – After a lengthy debate about your "Free bird care pack for every reader worth £20", I persuaded my wife that I am worth £20 and she has allowed me to send for it.

Bob Rundle
Camborne, Cornwall

My husband and I

SIR – If a member of the House of Lords marries a same-sex partner, what is the correct form of address for that partner? (Let's assume for the sake of simplicity that neither party's first name is Gaylord.)

N.C.
London W14

SHEDDING LIGHT ON A
PERFECT MARRIAGE

SIR – I was delighted to read the article on the great British shed because I have been championing its essential role in family life for years now.

In his teachings, the great mystic and spiritual teacher Osho once said: "To be alone is the only real revolution. To accept that you are alone is the greatest transformation that can happen to you."

So I explained to my wife that I really wanted her to experience this transformation and that to facilitate this I planned to buy myself a shed for her birthday, so that we could both dwell on Osho's teachings in peace. She agreed.

Incredibly, that was nearly 25 years ago now. Three children later we are more in love than ever – a state than can be summed up in a few short words: "I'm just popping down to the shed, darling, I shan't be long."

Basil Peabody
Playden, East Sussex

SNAKES AND MOTHERS

SIR – Your Letters page recently called into question the authenticity of both the tooth fairy and the Garden of Eden. I should have thought that most reasonable people would agree that the tooth fairy is, well, a fairy story. But backed by the authority of Genesis, the talking snake is certainly true (although I must admit that I have never met one; with the possible exception of my ex-wife's mother).

D.C.
Knutsford, Cheshire

HAPPY BIRTHDAY, MOTHER

SIR – Trying to buy a Christmas card for my mother I had great difficulty in finding one addressed to *Mother*. There were many to *Mum* or *Mummy*. I am now suffering the same problem in purchasing a birthday card and have been to 10 shops, all to no avail.

I feel it inappropriate for a sexagenarian son to send to his octogenarian mother a card addressed to *Mum* or *Mummy*. Am I the only person who feels this?

Bryce Mitchell
Chorleywood, Hertfordshire

WHEN I'M 73

SIR – I have finally come to the conclusion that my 73-year-old mother has become a born-again teenager.

She sleeps until all hours in the morning, never does any work and plays the television and radio far too loudly.

Her driving is atrocious (as is that of most of her friends), although she will never admit it or that she's ever in the wrong.

Her dress sense has stayed the same for so long it's actually come back into fashion.

Whenever I suggest something, she ignores it until one of her friends says exactly the same thing. Then it becomes a great idea.

Many of her friends drink far too much and they are nearly all on drugs (they would claim medical, not narcotic – but I reserve judgment on that).

All in all, I think she's just at that "difficult age".

Anon

SIR – A friend of mine remarked recently that he has reached an age that when he meets someone he has not seen for a while, the conversation always starts with an organ recital.

Peter Foston
Two Mile Oak, Devon

THE BIRDS, THE BEES
AND THE OAPs

SIR – I see that five-year-olds are now going to have sex education in schools. Could we please have adult sex education classes for those of us who missed out in our youth? There was certainly none at my county grammar school, even in biology.

I got most of mine from sex-starved Italian prisoners of war at a wartime school farm holiday camp, mostly by talk of the jig-a-jig variety.

The rest was just by trial and error – and great fun that was – but it would be nice to know for sure how my eight lovely grandchildren came about.

Geoffrey Geere
Abingdon, Oxfordshire

SIR – I recently received a spam email asking if I wanted to marry "a hot Russian chick". As I'm approaching 75 years of age and have blood pressure problems, I decided on this occasion not to accept this tempting offer.

Ivor Yeloff
Hethersett, Norfolk

SIR – As a pensioner whose assets are sagging, I am reluctant to put them on general view in the proposed new scanners at airports. I am therefore considering starting a business selling modesty pants and bras, with reflective foil inserts.

F. McG
Ispwich, Suffolk

SIR – In today's issue, the novelist Josa Young calls for "More sex please, we're grown-ups". While laudable in its intent, I feel that, as a gentleman in my mid-seventies who lives alone, I would ask for: "More sex please, we're elderly".

Mind you, I am sure that there are many in the same boat who would agree that even the chance would be a fine thing.

W. George Preston
Southampton

SIR – I have fond memories of conceiving my two sons and I hope that my wife does as well. The practice sessions were also pleasurable. Neither of my sons was heard to complain when they passed our genes on to the next generation.

However, the thought that my grandchildren or their progeny might be deprived of this simple pleasure because of laboratory generated sperm, as your report suggests, is appalling.

Pat Gadsby
Scleddau, Pembrokeshire

SIR – Your correspondent had roughly the right idea about which way to hang a Rothko. Whenever I plan to make love to a woman I always affix a newly completed painting on the ceiling so that she has something interesting to do during the process.

Peter Croft
Cambridge

SIR – Here is a different twist for St Valentine's Day: due to urinary problems I entered hospital on February 14 and had part of my reproductive system removed.

R.S.
Billericay, Essex

BIRTHING PAINS

SIR – I read your report that an attendant had shouted at a woman having a Caesarean: "F***** hell, why can't women in this hospital give birth naturally?"

That is nothing. While I was giving birth to my first son, two medical students were brought in to observe. I heard one say to the other, "Put you off sex for life, wouldn't it?"

Wendy McMullan
Cheltenham, Gloucestershire

SIR – As a former inspector of schools, I once talked to a Year 10 student who confided that she was pregnant. When I asked about the sex education she had received at school she claimed it had been thorough and informative. However, she added: "But you don't think about school when you're f******, do you?"

This is the best explanation I have heard for the failure of sex and relationship education to halt the rise in teenage pregnancies.

Shirley Elomari
Belle Vue, Shropshire

SIR – Isn't it about time sexual intercourse was banned in Britain under health and safety legislation?

A.S.
Yamaguchi, Japan

STAND BACK,
I'M A YOUNG PERSON

SIR – Jim White's article on turning 50 rang a few
bells with me and my colleagues. But if he thinks 50
is bad, try 60.

I'm sharper, wiser, more experienced and livelier
than many of those around me, but this is of no
consequence. If I stand by a photocopier mumbling
that it isn't working, someone will butt in with the
implication: "Stand back, I am a young person, I will
help you." Then they find that I am, in fact, right: it
is not working. But at least they have reassured me
that that is the case, for which I am grateful.

I know quite a lot, but I have had to explain to a
graduate that I was not born fully formed as I am
now; I was born a baby in the normal way, went to
school, went to college, knew nothing to start with,
but have picked up a lot along the way, including the
simple things they believe they should explain to
me. The young forget that we grew up during the
years of the development of, for instance,
computers, so they are not a mystery.

There are elements within the Fourth Reich – the
European Union – which want to take people over
70 off the road because they are perceived to be a
danger to others. That's seven years away in my case,
but I've just driven to the Dolomites and back with
no adverse consequences. In seven years' time I'd
like to think that I'd have the common sense not to

attempt it if I thought I wasn't capable. I wouldn't want some bureaucrat telling me I couldn't, based just on my age.

Despite pious noises by "caring" people against what they like to call ageism, there is an overall perception that anyone who is what I would call mature is over the hill, and should be treated as senile and patronised in a way that I sometimes find offensive. Usually, however, I laugh it off with the thought that they are simple folk who don't know any better.

To give Jim White hope, I have never in my life felt as confident and as buoyant as I do now. And if it all goes pear-shaped I have the exit door marked "Retirement".

Alan Mordey
Leamington Spa, Warwickshire

THE YOUTH OF YESTERDAY

SIR – Although it may seem unbelievable, I, a 15-year-old, wish to make a point about manners. I was taught from a very young age to thank people for simple niceties and to respond to a thank you with "You're welcome".

I exercise these two simple rules on a daily basis, so why is it that I am finding more and more adults who cannot?

It's all very well to complain about the rudeness of "the youth of today" but has anyone actually considered the manners of the youth of yesterday?

E.W.
Goxhill, North Lincolnshire

SIR – Can I look forward to a time when I can make a journey by public transport that doesn't include my having to request a young person to remove their feet from a seat?

W. Spragg
Thatcham, Berkshire

CHAPERONED BY A
FIVE-YEAR-OLD NEPHEW

SIR – When I go for a run (which is less often than it used to be) my natural route back takes me through the park, where there are slides and swings. This is the park where I played as a child and where I take my five-year-old nephew.

But now, I must be made to feel like a pervert for staggering back through the park after a run. So what should I do? Save my breath so I can keep running? Wear blinkers, so I can't look sideways in case I accidentally glance at some kids playing and remember my happy childhood? Is that illegal under New Labour?

Or perhaps I should take my five-year-old nephew with me? He can probably outrun me.

P.B.

FAT FAMILY CATS

SIR – I cannot describe the relief I felt when my human showed me the photograph in your newspaper of Orazi, the Italian cat who weighs 35 lb.

I am nagged interminably about my weight – and me a mere 15 lb! I have to be coaxed into the garden, and there I deign to run around a bit just to keep her happy.

I am even on a special diet, but I put my feet down firmly over the question of a weight clinic once a month.

What my owner doesn't seem to realise is that it's my genes – I mean, what's a girl to do? Anyway, I'm far too old now. If I lost weight my skin would just hang in folds, and that would be so unsightly.

> Yours, ever demanding food,
> **Hanzi**
> c/o Stalbridge, Dorset

FLAT FAMILY CATS

SIR – When our cat was run over by a woman driver I managed to catch up with her at the stop sign at the end of our street. When she wound down the window to inquire why I had stopped her, I noticed that she had a mug of coffee in one hand, an open newspaper on her lap and her windows were fugged up from morning condensation.

When I mentioned that she had just run over our cat she apologised profusely and said that she had not seen it.

Is this an example of female "multi-tasking", I wonder, or just another bad driver?

Sir Gavin Gilbey Bt
Dornoch, Sutherland

A LABRADOODLE IS NO DANDY

SIR – Your correspondents would appear to have a jaundiced view of Labradoodles and their owners. I live in the country. My owner's Wellington boots are black and scruffy (as am I). My village local welcomes everybody. I have no need of a Range Rover. A small hatchback is more than adequate for my needs and helps to reduce my canine footprint.

Bracken Fell (Aged 28 weeks)
Flintham, Nottinghamshire

An English dog's kennel is his castle

SIR – Is Parliament really planning to unleash whole packs of dog wardens to hound me in my own home? I beg to protest at this attempt to abolish canine rights of "Habeas Bonus", which include begging at the table and stealing anything edible I can get my jaws on – a law dating back in animal legend to the medieval dog owner, Maggie Carter.

Surely Parliament is barking up the wrong tree – and if I find that tree, I shall certainly cock my leg on it. An English dog's home is his kennel, if not his castle.

Psammutis (Pharaoh Hound)
c/o the Walkers
Warwick is my dog and bone

PS I am incredibly vain – would you like a picture?

Beware of the owner

SIR – I resent being told that, as a dog owner, I look like my pets. We have a brown Labrador and a Jack Russell. I do not resemble either of them. I look like an Alsatian.

Jeremy Woolcock
Great Bardfield, Essex

TELEVISION
AND RADIO

FORCIBLY RE-EDUCATED
BY THE BBC

SIR – Can I be alone in objecting to having re-education forced upon me by the modernist gauleiters of the BBC?

To escape the constant stream of feminist, or government-driven, sociology that infests almost every programme on Radio 4, I switched to Radio 3, hoping for a work from the canon of great composers. Instead I had to endure an eternity of meretricious dissonance from a living composer.

If I get in a taxi and ask for the National Gallery, I expect to be taken to Trafalgar Square and not to the Tate Modern. At least I can remonstrate with a cabbie.

Jeremy Macdonogh
Hoxne, Suffolk

SIR – I have found the perfect solution to your correspondent's problem concerning the bleatings of a garrulous female while eating breakfast. I simply avoid listening to *Woman's Hour*.

Colin V. Carter
Orpington, Kent

SIR – I have the odd feeling that I have been seeing far more of Nick Clegg, the Liberal Democrat leader, on BBC news than ever before.

Can it have anything to do with the Labour Government's decision to divert part of the licence fee away from the BBC and into other broadcasting expenses? Surely not.

Lydia Rivlin
London N10

CHANNEL-HOPPING MAD

SIR – In the evenings my wife and I spend 10 minutes trying to find something inoffensive on the television (tough, but it can be done) and then share a bottle of red wine.

I dare Gordon Brown to knock on my door and suggest I stop drinking for health reasons; it's the only thing keeping me sane.

Steve Baldock
Handcross, West Sussex

BRITAIN'S GOT NUDITY

SIR – Television channels have lost any morals and now consider half-naked females to be the ultimate sales technique: *Strictly Come Dancing*, for instance, or *Stars on Ice*. Don't these programmes have a dress code, apart from women in their underwear?

Likewise, I love my music but find it almost impossible to enjoy it on the television because the pleasure of melodic creativity indulging my ears is now blighted by video producers who clearly have a background in the XXX erotic arena.

When I was growing up there was a handful of top-shelf offerings and page-threes to titillate. Now in the age of the internet, lads' mags and MTV culture, sex, nudity and pornography are not just on every street corner but in every living room.

As parents of a seven-year-old girl and three boys, my wife and I are traumatised by the prospect of our children growing up in a society that is so immoral that sex has become the new super-brand.

Come on, Britain, put your clothes back on. If we don't take a moral stance the next generation will be rife with perverts, sex crime and underage pregnancies.

Yours Very Agitated
C.P.
Lincoln

SIR – As a young man I could never understand the point of steering a young woman backwards around a dance floor unless it was to achieve satisfaction later. The *Strictly Come Dancing* contests don't go far enough.

Robert Vincent
Wildhern, Hampshire

DOCTOR WHO?

SIR – The thought of a female Doctor Who is horrible. Each new doctor has been a reincarnation of the previous one, with all the mental abilities and memories of his predecessor. How, then, would such a doctor with the mind and brain of a man cope with all the physical and psychological attributes of a woman? Would he/she be able to ovulate? Lactate? Give birth? It is an abomination.

Jeff Best
London N14

HELEN MIRREN TO PLAY POL POT

SIR – Some people have said that an exact portrayal of Henry VIII is not important. But if it is important to portray Henry VIII as an attractive young man, then surely it is as important to portray him as the bloated tyrant he became?

What is the purpose of this latest BBC drama? Is it purely to entertain or does it help illuminate a particular period in this country's history?

And why stop at re-inventing an historical figure's physical appearance? Why not portray Hitler as a deeply caring, kind and totally misunderstood 6´3˝ blond Adonis or Joseph Stalin as a sensitive, mild-mannered Johnny Depp?

For that matter why not cast Helen Mirren as Pol Pot? I am sure it would make all of these dictators much more appealing.

J.M.

CROSSED WIRES

SIR – Having read the glowing reviews of *The Wire*, the new American series which several critics have called "the best series ever", my wife and I sat down to watch it with hopes of many enjoyable evenings to come.

After about 20 minutes, during which the F word appeared every five words, not to mention the various other expletives that were conjured up, we decided that we had had enough and turned the programme off.

Have standards now sunk so low in Britain that this sort of foul-mouthed material is considered acceptable?

A.G. Sellens
Old Bursledon, Hampshire

SIR – Following the hype you gave this programme, my wife and I decided we would try it. We almost jumped ship after 20 minutes but kept going until nearly the end. We then gave up. The plot seemed as though it might be good, but we really felt we would need subtitles to decipher all its nuances.

Was there also a sub-plot to see if any member of the forces of law and order could break the world record for the number of F words in one sentence? I certainly prefer our home-grown efforts.

Anthony Chapman
Morton, Lincolnshire

THE FOLLOWING TAKES PLACE IN BRITISH SUMMER TIME

SIR – It is a happy coincidence that Jack Bauer has returned to our screens in time for a new American president. His dynamic ability to solve his country's (and the world's) gravest problems is most reassuring.

On this side of the pond, though, we have the more cerebral Miss Marple, with her greater attention to detail. What a force for good in the world it would be if Mr Bauer and Miss Marple could work together.

Roger Bullock
Turnchapel, Devon

DELUSION AND THE CITY

SIR – *Sex and the City* worries me – and not just that I may be dragged kicking and screaming to see a chick flick. No, my concern is the effect it is having on women. The film and series portray four women, for the most part in late-middle-age, who can most kindly be described as of average looks.

In this world, they are portrayed as being able to pick up and put down good-looking, successful men who are significantly younger than they are. Among my friends, I have never seen anything remotely approaching this and unless New York operates on wildly different rules, it clearly doesn't represent any reality in the western world.

Now this is fine, provided women look to the film and series for a little escapism. After all, men have James Bond to fulfil the equivalent role. The difference is that the overwhelming majority of men know James Bond is escapism and represents little in the way of reality.

However, most of the women to whom I have spoken on the subject of *Sex and the City* see it as something of a life guide to which they should aspire. This is sad on the level of men who watch James Bond and then go out and buy a plastic gun and wear it to the office with a shoulder holster.

Come on, ladies, time for a reality check.

Phil Bailey
Crickhowell, Powys

NOISES OFF

SIR – I am not sure where it all started, but can we please rid the BBC's rugby coverage of female commentators? They have not the slightest idea what it is like to play the game, and so their comments are worth nothing.

Listening to ignorant money-earners is no replacement for listening to chaps who know what they are talking about.

Lt Col Dale Hemming-Tayler (retd)
Driffield, Gloucestershire

IT'S RAINING MEN

SIR – Watching television this week I was struck by the shape of the ladies announcing the local and national meteorological conditions. I thought that a suitable advertisement for the departments involved would be: "If you want to get pregnant become a weathergirl."

Peter Binder
Alderley Edge, Cheshire

SIR – I probably shouldn't even be thinking this but I can't help noticing a definite correlation between the drippyness of the television dolly bird "weathercasters" and the inaccuracy of their forecasts.

Tony Stone
Oxted, Surrey

DIRTY FLESH

SIR – There is a new male affliction and form of self-harm that has reached epidemic proportion. I refer, of course, to the ever-increasing amount of media, sports and entertainment industry men who, in the words of my old Colour Sergeant, "fail to get close to their razors".

I have taken counsel from my wife and two teenage daughters who promise me that what the aforementioned Non-Commissioned Officer also called "dirty flesh" is not remotely attractive or endearing to the opposite sex.

So why are there more and more males who wish to look like vagrants or park-bench dossers?

Nicky Samengo-Turner
Hundon, Suffolk

PUBLIC EXECUTIONS FOR BRAND AND ROSS...

SIR – So, Russell Brand and Jonathan Ross are to be suspended for their obscene phone calls. Hopefully it will be a public execution. No doubt there will be thousands of people, who live by decent moral standards, queuing up to observe the proceedings and hoping that a loud and clear message will be sent to the BBC that "enough is enough".

Ian Arnott
Kidderminster, Worcestershire

SIR – Cut off their goolies. Ouch!

Judith Rowe
London SW11

SIR – May I suggest that the most appropriate punishment for Messrs Ross and Brand, a scandalous pair of overgrown schoolboys, would be for them to be summoned to the BBC Beak's study where they would be invited to offer any mitigating reasons for their appallingly sick prank on Andrew Sachs.

In the absence of any good reasons, they should each receive "six of the best", old-fashioned style. Once the tears have stopped, this should be followed by a stern warning as to their future behaviour and the stoppage of any pocket money for at least the rest of the term.

Malcolm Burley
Painswick, Gloucestershire

PS I think Matt would have got here first had he not been on his hols.

SIR – Messrs Brand and Ross need a haircut. If there is a mess on the outside, there is a mess on the inside.

Judith Walker
Stanmore, Middlesex

SIR – S***! B******! F***! C***!

Do you think that the BBC will pay me to perform live with this material? If so they can go f*** themselves.

Mervyn Woodward
Ashwell, Devon

SIR – When I read about the obscene nature of this show, I was reminded of my early days in the Royal Navy. Any boy caught swearing was made to stand in front of his division and gargle with a disgusting mixture of soft soap, disinfectant and other such cleansers.

He then had to call out in a loud voice: "Ahoy, ahoy, ahoy, this will make me a clean mouth boy."

Perhaps the BBC could introduce something along those lines.

Trevor Coppock
Durham

SIR – I saw your photograph of Jonathan Ross and his family and couldn't help thinking what a little porker his daughter is. I told all my mates and they laughed so much they nearly p***** themselves. I bet not everyone would think it funny though.

N.G. Pedley
Matlock, Derbyshire

SIR – I have just heard that Kenneth Tynan used a vulgar four-letter word during a BBC television broadcast in 1965.

I should like to add my disapprobation to that of the thousands of others who have been shocked by his behaviour.

John A. Holland
Maidenhead, Berkshire

...BUT THE LADY'S DAUGHTER'S FOR BURNING

SIR –

In the Green Room they got very cross,
"Golliwog isn't on," said the boss.
Now the Beeb's shown no quarter
To Maggie T's delightful daughter,
But it's different for Jonathan Ross.

Geoffrey V. Willis
Halstead, Essex

SIR – I'm looking for a one-eyed Scottish golliwog I can send to the BBC. That'll get them in a tizzy.

Martin Horsfall
Newick, East Sussex

SIR – Am I alone in being offended by the PC brigade and other loony types arrogant enough to try to dictate which words we can or cannot use these days?

Those few remaining folk with common sense know that words are just words, and it can only be their context and style of delivery that sometimes cause offence.

I wish that they, and that other group, the gratuitously over-sensitive, whose affectation often causes me offence, would, in the words of Roger Daltrey, just f-f-f-fadeaway.

Bill Rushton
Soudley, Shropshire

SIR – Yesterday my daughter (British, blonde) was sitting on a train opposite another girl (British, black) who said audibly to her travelling companion: "She looks just like my Barbie."

My daughter replied: "And you look just like my golliwog."

Discuss.

P.T.E. Massey
Woodchurch, Kent

THE USES
AND ABUSES OF
LANGUAGE

PRESENT IMPERFECT
AMERICANISMS

SIR – Am I the only person who has noticed an increasing tendency in our country, particularly among advertisers, to use the simple past tense rather than the present perfect? For example, "Life just got better," rather than "Life has just got better."

This way of speaking may be perfectly acceptable if you are an American, but it sounds ugly to my English ears.

M. Harrison
Manchester

SIR – As Great Britain continues its slow and inexorable slide into Little America, could I make a plea, as a small token of resistance, for the elimination of one particularly irritating habit? I refer to the increasing use in everyday speech – particularly in teen-speak – of the redundant word *like*, as in: "He's, *like*, so awesome."

We all know that Americans talk a lot but say very little of substance, hence their need to interpose a word in order to allow their brains to catch up with their mouths. I would hope that parents and teachers could cooperate to rid us of this threat to what little is left of the English language.

David Young
Rotterdam, Netherlands

FAITHLESS GOVERNMENT

SIR – It is sad to see James Purnell, a Government minister, signing off his resignation letter to the Prime Minister simply "Yours".

Does this show a decline in standards, a lack of sincerity or in the case of this Government, perhaps both?

I am, Yours faithfully,
Barry Morgan
Horton Kirby, Kent

SIR – Am I alone in being bored by Government ministers stating: "We're doing all we can"?

Surely as taxpayers we should expect nothing less? Even if they cannot be specific, can they not think of something more imaginative to say?

Andrew Blake
Shalbourne, Wiltshire

SIR – On the *Today* programme the Chancellor referred to the financial sector as having "less institutions". Was this a Freudian slip or does he really not know the difference between *less* and *fewer*?

Andrew J. Morrison
Faveraye-Machelles, France

SIR – On television last Sunday morning I heard the Secretary of State for Health, a man who would like to be Prime Minister, use *infer* instead of *imply*.

Ted Shorter
Hildenborough, Kent

SIR – Could somebody please tell our Foreign Secretary how correctly to pronounce the word *harassment*?

Bill Swanson
Hampton, Middlesex

SIR – Our Government is fighting among itself while the country loses billions and yet my greatest – and I admit somewhat pedantic – bugbear is the shoddy speech from our most influential politicians, in particular their inability to pronounce words ending in "t" correctly.

Tony Blair began the trend (maybe in a cynical New Labour-esque attempt to "get down with the masses"). The current standard-bearers are too numerous to list in full. However, Hazel Blears and Jacqui Smith immediately spring to mind as the worst culprits in *Parliamen'*.

Philip Waddington
Blackpool

SHOCKING GRAMMAR

SIR – You recently recounted the story of the doctor who embarked on an affair with his receptionist. We read that when he was confronted by the cuckolded husband, he replied: "Me and your wife love each other."

I am struggling to decide whether I am more shocked by his morals or his grammar.

Nic Cookson
London SW18

SIR – Perhaps the writer of the pamphlet on swine flu should take a refresher course on the use of English. On page one, it says: "Keep this information safe." Surely it should be *safely* as it is an adverb.

On the following line it says: "to refer back". *Back* should be deleted as tautological.

John Platts
Manchester

SIR – A few years ago, a young secretary pinned a notice to the stationery cupboard stating, "If the stationary has run out please inform Janet." I underpinned this with a note stating, "If the stationery is stationary, then it has not run out, please tell Janet."

Michael McGinty
Elstree, Hertfordshire

SIR – Does London Underground hold the world record for the most commonly viewed grammatical error? Every carriage carries several signs stating: "It is an offence not to carry a valid ticket for your entire journey." Whereas what they mean, of course, is: "It is an offence not to carry a ticket valid for your entire journey."

What a difference the position of two words makes. If I carry a cup final ticket – a perfectly "valid" ticket – am I within the law?

Dr Keith Ray
Marlow, Buckinghamshire

SIR – The first sentence of the article on your science page today reads: "I'm not religious, but I have thought about religion all of my life."

Am I alone, I wonder, in being repeatedly irritated – and not in a small way – by the unnecessary use of the word *of* in this sentence?

So many people seem to misuse it thus – even the Pope. However, I can excuse him – not because I'm Catholic but because at least he is foreign and can therefore be excused.

Andrew Bartlett
Bracklesham Bay, West Sussex

CROSSED WORDS

SIR – The *Telegraph* crossword of October 24 served to univite the contents of our braincases, alength as they were, because it obliged us to indagate every lexicon at our disposal. We experienced dreamwhile and were not at all cheesed off while vying with each other in distinguishing the emys from the okapi. We felt that the compiler was being jestful and are hoping that the experience will not be ergodic.

Alan and Gillian Furse
Teignmouth, Devon

THE MOST TORTURED METAPHOR EVER WRITTEN?

SIR – Gordon Brown and Alistair Darling are living in cuckoo land. Neither knows whose egg they are hatching when they attempt to find a partner to aid them on the flight from the mess that they have got this country into.

Not a very loud cheep comes from the rookery of unions, nor the financial branches of commerce. Brown and Darling have to admit they are fledglings of a breed about to become extinct. Don't "do-do" anymore. Just resign.

T.D.
Bridlington, East Yorkshire

THE MOST TORTUROUS JOKES

SIR – I note that MI5 is to end its bar on homosexuals entering the service. Should these agents be deployed at Christmas, would they be Mince Pies?

> **R.J.**
> Sandgate, Kent

SIR – Is looking at photographs of the new MI6 chief in his swimwear speedophilia?

> **J.B.**
> Woking, Surrey

SIR – The Crown Prosecution Service is considering whether to bring charges against the culprits who stole the store name in St Ives. It would be Wool Worth it.

> **B.F.**
> Derby

SIR – How sad to read of Bernie Ecclestone's impending divorce from his wife. Is it because they have grown apart?

> **R.M.**
> East Grinstead, West Sussex

SIR – If swine flu ever manages to combine with avian flu will this be evidence that pigs really can fly?

> **M.B.**
> Chelmsford, Essex

SIR – If you think you've contracted swine flu, should you send for a hambulance or just put oinkment on the nasty rasher?

> **J.B.**
> Kineton, Warwickshire

SIR – On arriving at school for work yesterday I found a set of poor quality dentures, discarded by a visitor to the Hallowe'en disco the evening before. I can reliably inform you that fangs ain't what they used to be.

> **S.B.**
> Great Kingshill, Buckinghamshire

SIR – You recently reported that the Vice Mayor of Shanghai had been sentenced to a suspended death penalty. Does this mean that they will hang him?

> **S.L.**
> St Leonards on Sea, Essex

SIR – I suppose you could say that the Frenchman in your report who delayed a train when his arm was trapped in the lavatory has met his Waterloo.

J.M.S.
Shefford, Bedfordshire

SIR – Might the possible refinancing of the *Daily Sport* and the *Sunday Sport*, under discussion in the business section, not more accurately be described as tat-for-tit, rather than debt-for-equity?

J.A.
London SW18

SIR – The Large Hadron Collider, we are told, will not now be operational until springtime. Maybe the LHC has gone pineapple-shaped – in other words, a "Pina Collider".

W.G.P.
Southampton

SIR – With reference to the report of a leak of a ton of helium, perhaps the Large Hadron Collider should now officially be renamed the Large Hadron Colander.

M.H.
Smeeth, Kent

I AM BANNING THE WORD I

SIR – Today, I sat and read your Letters page and, as normal, set myself up for the disappointment of reading letters starting with the pronoun *I*.

What a delight to find that you printed the missive of not one correspondent who started with such a beginning.

Is it possible for you to repeat this feat every day?

Stuart C. McIntosh
Slaidburn, Lancashire

SIR – I read with utter disbelief and dismay the article regarding the suggestion by supposedly intelligent people that phrases like "old masters" and words like "immigrant" should be banned on the grounds of sexism or racism.

Fortunately the highly appropriate adjective "tossers" is not included on the banned list.

C.B.
Burton-in-Kendal, Cumbria

SIR – How refreshing to see that, in the politically correct society we have created for ourselves, we can still refer to a *black hole* in a financial context.

Lovat Timbrell
Saltdean, East Sussex

SIR – I wonder how many of your readers have noticed the increasing use of the word *impact* as a verb to describe almost any situation, where what is really meant is *affect*. As a result, impact is losing all its impact and a stronger word like *hit* may have to take its place.

Martin Paterson
Fittleworth, West Sussex

HELLO!

SIR – Despite an aristocratic descent (and have I ever descended), I'm not sure if I should say *hallo* (as per the *Today* programme) or is it *hello* (as per the magazine) or is it *hullo* (as we used to say at my school).

Halp!

Mervyn Woodward
Ashwell, Devon

AUTOCUE CONSPIRACIES

SIR – Am I the only person who is enraged on a daily basis by newsreaders pronouncing the word *decade* with the emphasis on the second syllable? Is there a conspiracy to change the pronunciation of every word over two syllables?

It used to be quite fun listening to a different pronunciation of *Chechnya* every evening on BBC One when that particular crisis was occurring, but now I find that I am quivering with fury and reaching for a restorative double gin whenever the next verbal abomination occurs.

Jane Brittain-Long
Newnham on Severn, Gloucestershire

SIR – Am I the only one to be annoyed by the growing number of newsreaders and presenters on the radio (and television as well, I presume) who pronounce the word *homage* so that it rhymes with the French word for cheese?

Who told them to do that? It is an English word, having entered the language from Old French in the Middle Ages. It is pronounced in the same way as *cottage*, or *forage*, both of which entered the language at a similar time.

Something must be done before I am successful in throwing my shoes at the radio.

Christopher Monniot
Crawley, West Sussex

SIR – Am I alone in hearing journalists saying *vunrubble* and *Guvvament*?

John Hodges
Woodstock, Oxfordshire

SIR – I am getting fed up with newsreaders saying "rather" and then correcting themselves when they make a mistake.

Why don't they say "Sorry"?

Hyder Ali Pirwany
Okehampton, Devon

SIR – Can somebody please explain why around 99 per cent of television and radio presenters pronounce *our* as *are*?

This is particularly annoying when the two words come together, such as Tim Wonnacott's posh voice on *Bargain Hunt* asking: *"Are are contestants gonna be able tuh find the bargains?"*

Furthermore, why do they all pronounce *been* as *bin*?

Does nobody monitor/train/correct these highly paid presenters? Or do they just have carte blanche?

Dave McConnell
Winchester, Hampshire

SIR – How pleasing it would be if BBC interviewers were (politely) to correct their subjects' grammatical slips. Perhaps a necessary preliminary might involve those interviewed politely pointing out corrections to their interviewers' howlers.

Ian Daglish
Alderley Edge, Cheshire

SIR – Why do people being interviewed always say "you know" in answer to a question? If we did indeed know, then we wouldn't be wasting our time listening to them. Gone, it would seem, are the good old days of the simple "er".

Russ King
London N11

UNSETTLING PUNCTUATION

SIR – The apostrophe, which you report is now under threat, may produce a mildly unsettling image. In Oxford, for example, I never felt wholly at ease entering St Helen's Passage.

Robert Stephenson
Henley-on-Thames, Oxfordshire

SIR –

The apostrophe is an important mark.
It is well used within a writer's art.
But now there are those who say, "Get rid!"
"What next," I ask "will be the bid?"
Shall we drop all punctuation marks?
Throw out English lessons for a start?
Become illiterate wholesale,
And have two lessons less to fail?
Or get rid of English, all well and good,
All because of an apostrophe misunderstood?

Georgina Boalch
North Weald, Essex

SIR – Following on from Bryony Gordon's article on Harry Potter, I would like to add that, some years ago, my daughter's primary school homework was to find examples of colons and semi-colons in books she knew. Since she was reading a Harry Potter novel at the time, we looked there first and there were none.

It took an older edition of Winnie The Pooh to find useful numbers of them.

I strongly agree, therefore, with Miss Gordon's negative view of Harry Potter.

Basil Steven-Fountain
West End, Surrey

Pnshng bd splng

SIR – I read with dismay your article on the use of text language in school essays. It makes one wonder about the demise of the red pencil.

In the 1950s, if there were three spelling mistakes in a paragraph, the paragraph was crossed out. If two paragraphs were crossed out the whole essay was rejected – occasionally with a trouser-warming thrown in for good measure.

Raith Smith
Sherborne St John, Hampshire

SIR – At my daughter's speech day, I was enormously impressed to hear the deputy headmistress announce that one of the girls had won the prize for "the best written work in history".

I only mention it in case there are other people out there slaving away on this task – forget it, the prize has already been awarded.

John Batting
Wargrave, Berkshire

ABSOLUTELY FAVOURITE
NEOLOGISMS

SIR – Am I absolutely your only reader who absolutely cannot understand why the word *absolutely* (invariably pronounced *apsolutely*) has absolutely permeated the English language in an absolutely pointless manner?

I do hope that the answer is not, "Yes, absolutely".

Andrew Blake

Shalbourne, Wiltshire

SIR – My favourite – as yet undetected – neologism of the last 20 years is a *fervert* – someone radicalised by any religion.

I know you won't print this, as you never do, but . . .

Jenny Cobb
Five Ashes, East Sussex

THE CREDIT CRUNCH

Not me, darling – Darling, darling

SIR – Am I alone in being blamed by my wife for not seeing the economic meltdown coming? Or are there other husbands out there in the same boat?

Michael Cattell
Mollington, Cheshire

Bankers' crimes and punishments

SIR – I am very angry because of the long fight I have had to get about 70 per cent of my deferred pension from a defunct company scheme.

I am very angry because I am still fighting for compensation for my damaged Equitable Life Pension scheme.

I am very angry because my other private pensions schemes have been damaged in the current financial tsunami.

I am very angry because the interest on my savings accounts is so low.

I am very angry that, after a lifetime of work and saving, I will probably end up living in penury.

I do not want justice; I want revenge.

I notice that rioters in Latvia tried to storm government buildings. I want that here now.

I want to rent Guantanamo Bay when it is empty

and fill it up with bankers and politicians.

I want rigorous interrogation techniques to get to the bottom of this toxic debt bubble and the utter failure of the regulatory authorities.

I want show trials.

I want it all.

John Carlin
Gedling, Nottinghamshire

SIR – With reference to your article about testing on animals, may I suggest a way round this thorny issue? I propose that we use bankers instead of white mice. After all, there are now more bankers than white mice, people can become attached to white mice and there are some things that even a white mouse will not do.

Mark Duhig
Tunbridge Wells, Kent

SIR – The parable in Matthew 18: 23–35 comes to mind: a servant was remitted a debt of ten thousand talents and immediately committed to prison a fellow servant, who owed him one hundred pieces of silver.

May the bankers be handed over to be tortured until their debt is paid.

Brian Kearney
Charlton Kings, Gloucestershire

SIR – Is the Prime Minister not useless if, with a huge parliamentary majority and broad cross-party support, he cannot bring greedy and unrepentant bankers to heel?

It makes one despair of democracy. In a totalitarian system like China, instead of bonuses they would have each received a bullet in the back of the head, had their ill-gotten wealth seized and their families made to pay the price of that bullet.

Dr Yen-Chung Chong
Brighton

SISTER, CAN YOU SPARE A THOUGHT?

SIR – Judith Woods says we should spare a thought for those city wives who used to enjoy daily blow drys, houses in Notting Hill and chateaux abroad, and now have to call in tears to cancel the services of underpaid Brazilian cleaners and change their airline tickets to economy.

So I did: "Ha, ha, ha, ha, ha, ha, ha."

M.W.

THE NAME BLAME GAME

SIR – To my mind, the whole thing began to unravel when the system fell into the hands of people with names like Tom, Fred and Andy. We had the right idea with Eddie George at the Bank of England. When they knighted him, we all called him Sir Edward, and the system ran quite well thereafter.

Adrian Williams
Headington, Oxford

GOTCHA, ICELAND!

SIR – If the Icelandic government continues to procrastinate about monies owed to our savers and councils by their banks, Gordon Brown should evoke the Falkland spirit and send a crack unit of our finest binge-drinkers to Reykjavik.

After about a week of causing wanton damage and mayhem in the city centre, the Icelanders will soon realise that you don't mess with the Brits.

Ivor Yeloff
Hethersett, Norfolk

SIR – Would it, I wonder, be possible to ask that Iceland repay the deposits in fish rather than money? If so, the councils involved would be able to ensure that school dinners were mostly made up of fish.

Recalling my grandmother's advice about eating fish to improve brainpower this would surely (and quite quickly, given the amounts involved) increase the IQ of schoolchildren in their respective areas.

It would also, I suggest, be much to the envy of those councils who did not take up the interest rates on offer in Iceland.

Rodney Galpin
Reading, Berkshire

SIR – Those Icelandic bankers are turning out to be rather dodgy geezers.

Tom Knowles
London SW10

MONTY PYTHON AND THE STOCK EXCHANGE

SIR – Seeing the gutless panic in the stock market, am I the only one reminded of "Brave Brave Sir Robin" in *Monty Python and the Holy Grail*?

Nigel Price
Marple Bridge, Cheshire

SIR – Am I the only one to see the obvious solution to the current downward spirals in the world's stock markets? Switch off all the computers. Insist that all share dealings are based on real decisions and real trades made by real people, assessing the real worth of a business, and not by obeying the follow-my-leader software constructs of some obscure tracker programme, designed and tested during the boom years by a struggling PhD in Economics student over a half-eaten kebab in an Islington bed-sit.

David Powell
Saunderton, Buckinghamshire

WHEN THE RECESSION HITS HOME

SIR – Am I the only one mystified as to why, in the current trough of recession, shops in South Kensington are able to charge more for baguettes and cappuccinos?

John Hine
London SW5

SIR – Given that we are all going to be taxed to death for the next 20 years, I'm tempted to send my CV to the Somali pirates to see if they'll take me on as a trainee. I may not live as long, but at least if I reach retirement age, I'll be able to afford to eat.

Phil Bailey
Crickhowell, Powys

SIR – We hear the news that there is a "critical" shortage of sperm donors. On the same day Government figures state that unemployment is rising fast.

Is the solution not obvious? Or are Government ministers spending too long behind closed doors themselves?

Nik Cookson
London SW18

SIR –

How we roared
While our house values soared.
Bankers were heroes,
Frothing the zeroes,
Now we can't see for dust.
Those we did trust.
We knew it was voodoo,
But what would you do?
You can't feel betrayed
By a piper you paid.

Andrew Schofield
London SE1

CHRISTENING THE
TAXPAYERS' BANKS

SIR – When the dust finally settles on the merger of Halifax Bank of Scotland and Lloyds, I expect a suitable name for the newly created banking giant will have to be chosen.

Might I suggest: Bank of Scotland/ Lloyds/ Halifax. For trading purposes, this could be conveniently abbreviated to: BoLloX

> **James L. Shearer**
> Edinburgh

SIR – May I suggest Lloyds TSB and HBOS be called Bolshy SOBs Ltd?

> **Roger Brady**
> Bad Schwalbach/Ramschied, Germany

SIR – My wife asked me today why the Government was nationalising Bed and Breakfasts.

> **A.S.**

SIR – Is it true that the Origami Bank in Japan has folded?

> **Graham Fields**
> Barnham, West Sussex

SIR – I heard on the radio that the German finance minister had criticised our Prime Minister for "tossing around billions". Was the last word necessary?

Robert Frogley
Carshalton, Surrey

SIR – I am absolutely appalled that Northern Rock have the audacity to pay their employees bonuses after being bailed out by the taxpayer. I have therefore changed their name somewhat:

Not
Only
Robbing
Taxpayers
Hairbrained
Executives
Raid
Northern
Rock
Of
Capital.
Keds.

(Keds are bloodsucking insects.)

John Cartwright-Tickle
Costa Blanca, Spain

SIR –

City
Arbitrageurs
Perform
Inexcusable
Tricks
And
Lose
Investors
Serious
Money

Bankers' bonuses
And
Incompetence
Leave
Others
Utterly
Terrified

Bob Matthews
Tisbury, Wiltshire

FLOWERS OF SCOTLAND

SIR –

Royal Bank of Scotland.
Halifax Bank of Scotland.
Gordon Brown of Scotland.
Alistair Darling of Scotland.
Fred the Shred of Scotland.

Geddit? Luckily for them, there'll always be an
England (but beware the anger of a patient man).

David Myles
Wingerworth, Derbyshire

SIR – After so many years of the Scottish Raj
continually adopting the moral high ground in both
national banking and politics, am I alone in taking
pleasure at their downfall?

Philip Congdon
La Bastide d'Engras, France

DEAR FRED THE SHRED

SIR – I am concerned about my savings, some of which are deposited with the Royal Bank of Scotland. I wonder if I might write to the Chairman and Chief Executive as follows:

Dear Goodwin,

As you know, you have borrowed a substantial sum of money from me ("the Loan") to fund your business. Recent events, however, have given me considerable cause for concern as to the viability of your company and therefore the security of the Loan. While I appreciate what you say about the assistance given to you by your guarantor, Her Majesty's Chancellor of the Exchequer, I imagine that he will have been giving guarantees to others who have also lent to your bank and to your competitors.

In the circumstances I am therefore writing to notify you of the changes that I am making to the terms of your loan. With effect from close of business on Thursday October 16 ("the Default Date") the rate of interest payable on your loan will increase to 10 per cent above the Bank of England's Base Rate, the interest to be payable fortnightly in arrears. I also require security in the form of a Legal Charge (to be Registered at HM Land Registry) over your premises at 1 Fleet Street, London, EC4 ("the Premises"), the Charge to be in place by close of business on the Default Date. My valuer will be attending the Premises to do a valuation at 8.30 a.m. on October 14 and I should be grateful if you would ensure that he has unrestricted access throughout the Premises as necessary.

As well as meeting your own legal costs, you will be responsible for my legal costs and an arrangement fee of five per cent of the loan.

In normal circumstances I would be content for you to add the arrangement fee to the loan but in this case you should let me have a draft drawn in favour of The National Bank of the People's Republic of China which my agent will collect from you at close of business on the Default Date.

If you are unable to meet all of these terms by close of business on the Default Date then you should arrange a draft (payable as above) for the balance outstanding on the Loan (including closing interest) to be ready for collection at that time.

Finally, I would like to say how much I have valued our business relationship over the years and that I regret having to bring it to an end in this way. With your experience of business affairs you will, I am sure, appreciate the need for me to protect the interests of myself and my family and I wish you and your shareholders well for the future.

Charles Boscawen
Dennington, Suffolk

CREDIT CRUNCH – I TOLD YOU SO

SIR – In late February 2008 I sent a four-page
financial report written by myself in March 2000 to
each of the 15 Bank of England members on the
Monetary Policy Committee. The report predicted
the present situation facing the world.

To my letter I added the following PS: "The
world could be sitting on the brink of a systemic
financial meltdown."

Needless to say, not one member replied.

David Tolhurst
Whepstead, Suffolk

SIR – As you can see I submitted this letter, which
you did not publish, over a year ago, in April 2008.
With hindsight it seems uncannily prophetic.

"On yesterday evening's BBC News it was
reported that Gordon Brown intends to concentrate
on the current problems in the British economy.
Now we're for it!"

Ron Mason
East Grinstead, West Sussex

CREDIT CRUNCH – DOESN'T EXIST

SIR – Without the hysterical media coverage there would be no credit crunch, recession or anything worse. In 1899, during the Boer War, it took four months for news to get back to Britain – what a blessing!

Bob Wydell
Oswestry, Shropshire

SIR – It seems to me that the current economic crisis is being worsened by certain areas of the press. A few commentators are worse than others, and some certainly leave me with a growing *Pestonmism* about the whole thing.

Mark Downs
Leigh, Lancashire

SIR –

"ALL personnel at 'MI6'.
Thought there was a 'Credit Crunch'.
When there HASN'T been.
It was just Gordon 'Gold Stealer' Brown.
Trying to 'nick' money from The Treasury.
For his MATES.
In 'New Labour'.
And to try to get Cherie Booth.
Elected as Prime Minister.
One day".
"Uncle?".
"Say nothing!".
"'Duffers'!".
'MI6'
THE SECRET INTELLIGENCE SERVICE
cc The British State
'MI6'
GCHQ
22 SAS
'The Circus'

M

LAW AND
DISORDER

HE'S A POLICEMAN,
GET US OUT OF HERE

SIR – OK, I confess, I have been watching *I'm a Celebrity* on ITV. Amid the nonsense of boobs and sleeping arrangements, there is one revelation that is extremely worrying: Brian Paddick has shown why the police force has lost so much public confidence and has moved itself outside the community it is supposed to protect.

The man is a complete waster who seems to think that every "situation" needs debate and an "understanding" of all parties. What a wet, limp idiot! And he rose to the higher ranks! Small wonder the rest of the force does what the hell it wants.

Lt Col Dale Hemming-Tayler (retd)
Driffield, Gloucestershire

SIR – Like many elderly pensioners I have, in the past, been fearful of going out at night. Had I done so, and had the misfortune of meeting a group of young binge drinkers, I would have been "genuinely fearful of immediate or imminent mortal danger".

However, I am no longer afraid. It now appears to have been clearly established by the de Menezes case that, in such circumstances, without fear of prosecution or other repercussion, I can simply shoot the bastards.

Gerald Payman
Tenbury Wells, Worcestershire

SIR –

If you can keep your head while all about you
Offer violence to promote their simplistic view;
If you can smile and show forbearance,
While others spit, and snarl and threaten you;
If you can stand in one thin line awaiting
The violence you must know must come;
Or turn your cheek despite the baiting,
Then do your duty, and join the Met, my son.

> **Malcolm Allen**
> Berkhamsted, Hertfordshire

WHO LET THE EXTREMISTS IN?

SIR – Gordon Brown and his fellow fascists have given themselves the right to imprison us without trial or charge for 42 days. Apparently, this is needed because there are thousands of terrorists in this country.

Well, I did not let them in, so who did?

> **Peter Howell**
> Malmesbury, Wiltshire

SIR – Your picture of Abu Qatada, the radical Muslim cleric, on a shopping expedition shows him carrying a 16-pack of lavatory paper. Does that mean that western ways are triumphing?

> **D. McC**
> London W14

HANGING'S TOO GOOD FOR THEM

SIR – In the absence of the death penalty I suggest that a punishment that may be a sufficient deterrent for knife and gun crime would be surgical castration. This would have the added advantage that aggression in the individual would be reduced and also that his genes would not be transmitted to future generations.

It has two disadvantages: it would not apply to women, but they do not figure largely in this crime; and it would be irreversible. Yet compared with the death penalty the man would still be alive.

> **A.B.B.**
> Dorset

SIR – Recent reports suggest a proliferation in society of feral, criminal teenagers. Since no malaise can be cured by treating merely the symptoms, should not our Government now be debating the wisdom of retaining the universal right to breed?

> **P.T.**

SIR – If the Government were serious about ending knife crime, it could do so in a week. All that would be necessary would be for anyone found with a knife, without proper excuse, to receive 10 lashes with a cat o'nine tails.

Fear is what prevents offences. Liberal do-gooders have got us into the mess we are now in, and that has got to stop.

R.R.

ALTERNATIVE ENERGY

SIR – If your correspondents want effective community penalties, let them put their minds to persuading our Home Secretary that long treadmills, worked by shifts of prisoners, would be an ideal way of filling the gaps in power generation that are increasingly being forecast.

An early release programme could be planned against aggregate numbers of megawatts of output. Green energy via hard manual work, applying old technology, at comparatively trivial cost and offering a two-fold benefit to the nation – who has got a better idea?

Bernard J. Seward
Bristol

SHOCK AND WAR

SIR – I was once again plunged into sadness at the news this evening of the deaths of three of our young servicemen in Afghanistan. God rest their souls.

But I have a question. When we hear the full, and quite proper, tributes from military spokesmen, why can't we hear an addendum, possibly something to the following effect:

"We will hunt down and kill those people who have killed our young men. We shall do so remorselessly and implacably. Our vengeance will also extend uncompromisingly to those who harbour or shield the killers of our young men. We have the firepower, and we will use it without mercy."

Isn't it time we started talking their language?

Perhaps then they may begin to understand where we stand. So stop this pussyfooting about. This is war, for God's sake; one even gets blood on one's handkerchief.

Anthony Wallace
Brighton

LOVE AND WAR

SIR – I am sorry, but as randy as the male Chelsea Pensioner may feel, I do think that feminism and political correctness have swayed the Board of Commissioners of the Royal Hospital Chelsea beyond reason in allowing them a bit of female company.

A couple of scarlet birds who manned a barrel for a few months in the Second World War (and who ultimately picked up a few pennies in gratitude) do not really equate to a dedicated professional soldier handing over 20-odd years or more in full pension.

Lt Col Dale Hemming-Tayler (retd)
Driffield, Gloucestershire

THE ROYAL AIR FLIRT

SIR – The decision by Prince William to switch his commission to the RAF makes good sense, especially where his private life is concerned. I doubt the Royal Navy would have anything suitable afloat that would allow him to visit West Berkshire so easily.

Robert Vincent
Wildhern, Hampshire

Naval standards

SIR – I find it difficult to believe that the Royal Navy has a serving captain with the first name of Wayne (report, June 17). Please do not tell me that he is married and that his wife is called Waynetta.

John Green
Hayling Island, Hampshire

Mrs Dumas is the head of MI6

SIR –

There is 'talk'.
Of a man.
Becoming 'C'.
Noooooo . . .
'Mrs. Dumas'.
Is 'C'.
And will REMAIN so.
Until I say otherwise.
As for 'The Usual Suspect'.
He will be 'vetted'.
Until his 'eyes bleed'.
If he is KGB.
He will be 'thrown to the dogs'.
If he is 'kosher'.
His 'application' to be a future 'C'.
Will have been 'noted'.

That's all.
cc The British State
UK Records
'MI5'
GCHQ
22 SAS
'The Circus'
'MI7'
'D'
'MI6'
'C'
'The Village'
'Number 1'
'The Dungeon'.
'The Farm'
The United Nations
'Interpol'
CIA

    M

SIR –
My choice
For the next Commissioner Of Police Of The
Metropolis?
Cressida ****.
She just needs to visit Oxford to have dinner with
The Master.
Like 'Harold Abrahams' does in 'Chariots Of Fire'.
To be 'corrected'.
On a few points.
Like 'attitude'.
cc The British State
'MI5'
'MI6'
GCHQ
22 SAS
'The Circus'

    M

SIR –
Oh dear …
I hope 'Dame' Stella Rimington.
Hasn't ordered her 'Boys'.
To 'Dump For England'.
In public 'loos'.
Like Eliza Manningham-Buller once did.
Because THAT.
Would be 'unfortunate'.
cc The British State
'MI5'
GCHQ
22 SAS
'The Circus'

M

TOM DALEY, CIA SPY

SIR –

'Tom' Daley.
'14 year-old'.
'Genius Diver'.
Looks like he MAY be a CIA 'Double'.
Though the 'Double' MAY be Canadian.
Probably 17 years old.
Look at page 55 of the 'Sport' section.
And THINK 'Jim Carrey'.
The mother?
MOTIVE?
Probably MONEY.
cc The British State
'MI5'
GCHQ
22 SAS
'MI6'
FCO

    M

~~~~~~~~~~~~~~~~~~~~~~~~~~~

This iPlus Freemail has been sent to you by someone
using an online iPlus Point at Union Street, Bristol.

DEAR DAILY
TELEGRAPH

A QUIVER FULL OF COMPLAINTS

SIR – It's the sort of thing I would expect from the BBC but I was appalled by your article on the Samurai horse archer on page 18 today.

Twice in the few lines beneath the picture you refer to "fire". I would have thought that a quality paper like yours would know that you never *fire an arrow* but *loose an arrow* and *shoot a bow*. At a push I suppose *shoot an arrow* would have been acceptable.

> **G.R. (a disgruntled archer)**
> Normandy, Surrey

SIR – Could you please, *please* refrain from putting staples in the centre of the Sports page. I use old newspapers when cleaning out my rabbit's hutch and would hate for her little paws to get caught in these.

(You may print my letter if you so wish; it might make someone smile. God knows we need a bit of humour.)

> **M.K.**

SIR – I am getting sick and tired of the *Telegraph's* abusive language towards animals: please stop referring to them as it as if they were objects. It is neither grammatically nor biologically correct to do this. Abuse starts with the mentality that animals are "things".

Here is the sentence I am referring to: "Crows attacked a kitten after it [sic] was left clinging to the upper branches of a tree."

I am moving to a paper which has more compassion – most probably *The Independent*.

Goodbye.

S.A.

SIR – If the fact that J.K. Rowling is scared of spiders is news, I thought you might like to know that one of my ducks is sick and I think I'm running out of milk.

Kevin Mann
Goodwood, West Sussex

HOW BIG IS A DINNER PLATE?

SIR – Despite being overwhelmed by festive emotions and enjoying the sight of carolers happily plying their trade and dodging shrapnel in the lanes and byways of north-east Hampshire, I am moved to compose this letter of complaint. I do so with charitable motives. No one can accuse me of being less than generous in sharing my wisdom.

I refer to an article headed, "Spider as big as a plate among scores of new species found in Greater Mekong". Despite the fact that the article itself goes on to stipulate that the plate at issue was a dinner plate, I feel that this is a wholly unsatisfactory comparison.

You see, my dear sir, many of us do not limit our mealtime habits to always ensuring that our crockery is of standard dimensions. In short, I have no idea what size a "dinner plate" is. Come supper time, chez moi, a plate is chosen according to my appetite. I suspect that the resulting choice would be larger than any arthropods known to science, be they south-east Asian or not.

I hope that you take note of my concern, and address this issue. If not, I fear that my next missive will be as long as an under-butler's cummerbund.

V.S.
Kingsley, Hampshire

New layout, new dangers

SIR – Your new layout has caused the first row in our household in 46 years of blissful marriage.

Please, *please* put the Sudoku on separate pages again so that normal relationships can be restored and we can each try our skills over the cornflakes.

Geoff Morton
March, Cambridgeshire

SIR – It has been a long-held ambition of mine to visit every place listed in the *Telegraph's* daily weather reports. With retirement approaching, I sat down on Sunday and plotted a route around Britain's towns and cities. Europe and the rest of the world would have followed.

Two days later, my plans and dreams are in tatters. At a stroke, your new-look weather page has made the task three times more arduous, if not impossible. I cannot, for example, find the Isle of Skye anywhere in my atlas, and I have been unable to decipher the initials MRSC which follow Bridlington.

Ah well. Back to the drawing board for me.

John Honeywell
Hook, Hampshire

HOLD THE FRONT PAGE

SIR – Has anyone found, while driving, a bigger
contrast between the traffic reports of BBC Radio
Stoke and those of BBC Radio Leicester?

G.J.
Birmingham

SIR – I don't know whether you include such news
but a remarkable coincidence occurred last Saturday
when two brothers, one at Eton, the other at
Ludgrove, both scored 114 not out in their respective
school matches.

Howzat?

A.L.
Shropshire

SIR – Would it be possible for my husband to make a
one-off guest appearance in your birthday column?
He always reads this first, with great interest,
followed by "deaths", with great relief not to be
mentioned.

He is a businessman, 64, and noted for his
signature bow tie.

B.C.
Essex

SIR – I would like to submit a story to be considered for an editorial in your newspaper: I have designed a flag to be potentially purchased for use as a world flag. A world flag is important as it recognises and symbolises that we are one. Its colours are universal, calling on all nations for peace and unity.

The design elements that represent the "flag of the world" are: our planet earth; a large star; a small star and the sun's rays in a golden yellow colour.

N.S.
Melbourne, Australia

SIR – I have come to know the biggest secret of MI5, CIA and Mossad regarding the torture of prisoners in Guantanamo Bay. Waterboarding is only a cover up for the real torture there, which now takes place by use of a microchip. The microchip is inserted via the ear into the brain of the suspect. It is extremely small – almost the size of a rice grain.

The microchip can then be used to control each and every movement of the terror suspect. He can be made to walk in front of a moving vehicle and get himself killed. He can be made to take a gun and kill people that MI5, CIA and Mossad want him to kill.

The range of the microchip is anywhere in the globe. Thus the CIA can control suspects in Afghanistan from their office in the Pentagon.

The speech of the suspects can also be controlled via the microchip and the suspect can be made to accept responsibility for crimes he has not done.

Suspects can be made to yell out, "I hijack this plane," while travelling.

The microchip can also be used to reduce the immunities to any particular virus or bacteria.

I request that you look into this matter.

Anon

THE LETTERS DESK CUPID

SIR – I read that Cameron Diaz believes that women fear being shunned if they say they do not want to have children.

I have, on occasion, imagined starting a family with Miss Diaz, but didn't mention it for fear of being shunned. Coincidentally, like Miss Diaz, I also never say never. I enclose my address and telephone number in case you hear anything.

Donald Keir
Dyce, Aberdeenshire

SIR – I do hope that the lady driver who nearly collided with me on the A338 near the Wiltshire/Berkshire border this morning, because she was using a mobile phone while looking at something on her lap, is still alive to read this.

Andrew Blake
Shalbourne, Wiltshire

PLEASE CENSOR MY HUSBAND

SIR – One of your correspondents derides David Cameron for engaging Carol Vorderman to investigate mathematics education policy. Personally, I would love to do some multiplication with Miss Vorderman.

Robert Warner
Aston, Oxfordshire

SIR – Since you reported the impending opening of a lap dancing club here in Henley-on-Thames I have organised new glasses and a blood pressure check with my doctor. I can't wait.

Robert Warner
Aston, Oxfordshire

SIR – Please stop publishing letters from my husband, Robert: after three in less than a fortnight, he is insufferable and has now taken to reading the Letters page online at 2 a.m. in order to get his oar in first.

Enough is enough, especially as there are still lawns to mow, leaves to sweep and logs to split.

Anne Warner
Aston, Oxfordshire

MR POOTER WRITES

SIR – I have bought *The Daily Telegraph* every day for at least 45 years and have written letters of comment to you several times. You have never published any of my letters and I am wondering what I have done to offend you.

I write for the *Hornby Collector* and *Model Rail Magazines* and they always publish my letters/articles. What am I doing wrong? Please help, dear editor.

A Loyal Reader

SIR – Over the past couple of years, I have probably sent, on average, 100 letters per year (roughly two per week) to *The Daily Telegraph*, covering matters of national security and local triviality.

I have had one published, and its content was so pathetic that I cannot even remember it. Why do xxxx *[name withheld. Ed.]* and xxxx get so many of their letters published? I presume they are "literary folk" with kudos, not that I have heard of either of them, apart from in *The Daily Telegraph*.

P.E.
Ripon, North Yorkshire

SIR – Why are my emails no longer published? Have I been banned? I am a Chartered Engineer!

J.D.

SIR – I noticed yesterday that out of 21 letters printed, 15 were from the south of England.
Any comments?

S.U.
Addingham, West Yorkshire

HOT-UNDER-THE-COLLAR RAMBLINGS

SIR – Having re-read my ramblings I am certain this will not be published as it doesn't quite deal with the point. I wish therefore to withdraw the letter but imagine that this is academic in any case. Many thanks, and I shall try to desist from this irritating habit of drafting hot-under-the-collar ramblings only then to have to withdraw them.

A.F.
Chesterfield, Derbyshire

SIR – My apologies. The email sent to you was meant for *The Cumberland and Westmorland Herald*. I pressed the wrong key, I guess.

I now appreciate how some people get into trouble. Again, sorry for the trouble.

D.C.
Longridge, Lancashire

RETURN TO SENDER

What a wet start to the day, trust that you got into work without getting too wet. Helen, I will let you have the chauffeur's hat back when we see you next.

Have a good day.

Love Dad xx
(ORIGINAL MESSAGE)

I sincerely apologise for addressing an email to you a little while ago, it was meant for my daughters. However, I in my old age managed to press the incorrect button.

A.A.

Dear Mr A,
No problem at all. I do hope they got into work without getting wet.

The Letters Desk

Good day dtletters@telegraph.co.uk ,
Your e-mail was found on the internet as specifically
being with Boy Scouting.

SIR – We are given to understand that you are
potential buyers of chemical fertilizer. We are an
exporter of chemical fertilizer in China. If you want
to purchase other fertilizers, such as urea, phosphate
fertilizer, please contact us too.

We look forward to receiving your early inquiries.

A.C.

A REQUEST FOR OUR THEATRE CRITIC

SIR – I would like to inform Mr Charles Spencer
that Scarlett Johansson (actress) is actually a clone
from the original person – Scarlett Galabekian – who
has nothing to do with her acting career. The clone
was created illegally by using stolen biological
material. The original person is very nice (not sexy),
and most importantly, a Christian young lady.

This is just a warning, because the original
person is not happy with these movies, images,
video, rumours etc. spreading.

As such, it would be really nice if we could all try
to slow down that "actress's" career development.
The original Scarlett will really appreciate that.

All clones needs to be returned to the original

family's control in Los Angeles. Do not wait until an FBI agent gives you a call with questions.

Original Scarlett was not engaged, by the way.

Her close friend Serge G

P.S.

LET'S ABOLISH EVERYTHING

SIR – Isn't it time we abolished: knighthoods and peerages (bribery), the Liberal party (politics), the offside rule (football), funding for faith schools (education), futures and options (shares), political correctness (dishonesty), the licence fee (BBC) and *may* and *could* (journalism)?

Bernard W. Roberts
Greasby, Wirral

ANSWERS, PLEASE

SIR – In these days of questions with few reliable answers, could somebody please help me solve the following problems?

When the large, end crust from a loaf is so delicious, why are the crusts on the edges of a sandwich so dry and inedible? Why do men stand in front of magazine racks elbow to elbow so that I can't get to the publications without shouting "Excuse me" in a very determined voice? Why does the tallest, broadest person in any audience always sit in front of me so that my husband and I have to do a little shuffle in order for me to see anything?

Lastly, and this is the most aggravating problem of all, why does the type on the top half of the newspaper always run below the fold so that in order to read the last two lines of a paragraph, one has constantly to lift the bottom edge?

Answers would be so welcome. Thank you.

Maggie Tur
Axbridge, Somerset

SIR – Nothing is simple.

Jack Palmer
Weymouth, Dorset

P.P.S.

Dear Mr Hollingshead,

Thanks so much for your kind letter about the forthcoming book, which you rashly propose to make worse than it need be by including one of mine.

I note your comment that you could "easily make two or three interesting Letters pages each day", so many printable offerings do you receive.

Well, why not? It's a great idea. A good Letters page is compulsive reading, and compulsive reading is compulsively read. Advertising follows readers.

I write as an old Fleet Street hack who edited one or two Letters pages back in hot metal days, and is fond of them on principle. Through them readers talk to their newspaper and to each other. I suggested to a couple of editors that their Letters pages were worthy of expansion, and received a sneer of cold command for my pains. *Neither of those fools has survived*.

May I beg you to consider running the idea past Will Lewis? Point out that to say No will leave him accursed like —— —— of the —— —— who said No too and now, if rumour does not lie, scrabbles for peanuts as a radio disc-monkey.

Kind regards,
Nick Guitard

Dear Iain Hollingshead,
Thank you for your letter telling me that you intend to include one of my unpublished letters in your forthcoming collection.

Which one of the many I have no idea – perhaps the one about resembling one's pets – but in any case I'm delighted. And of course I'll buy a copy. Several, probably.

After God knows how many years of writing letters, I had no success until May this year when you published my letter about the British media ignoring the 150th birthday of Jerome K. Jerome. That in turn led to a splendid feature about Jerome by the fragrant Celia Walden.

And now another letter is to be enshrined in print. But I still don't think I've cracked the code that guarantees publication.

With best wishes,
Jeremy Woolcock

Dear Mr Hollingshead,

I was delighted to receive your letter telling me that you are going to use one of my letters in your book. I will be doubly delighted to purchase a copy when it is published, if for no other reason than to let it lie open at the appropriate page for my husband to see. Councillor Stuart Boalch has been a daily reader of *The Telegraph* for over 15 years and has written several letters for the Letters page, none of which have been published.

It is strange how hazel eyes can look green in certain light, don't you think?

Georgina Boalch